PRAISE FOR ACT LIKE A SALES PRO

"*Act Like a Sales Pro* brilliantly blends acting and improv skills with sales tactics for a winning combination. Julie's ideas are great fun, effective, and easy to apply—even for non-actors like me! Follow the sales advice and exercises in this book and you'll soon be outperforming and outselling your competition."

—Dessie Fafoutis, senior marketing manager, CaridianBCT

"There is an overwhelming volume of sales advice available today, however there are very few authors who approach the topic of sales in a unique and fresh way, which is why we are fans of Julie's work."

—Nicole Lombard, production director, *Entrepreneur* and *ThinkSales* magazines, South Africa

"This book should be on every real estate agent's desk. Hansen shows agents how to enhance their authentic selves for both client and agent successes!"

—Laura Dirks, author of *Marketing Without Mystery*, and real estate broker, Coldwell Banker Devonshire.

ACT LIKE
A SALES PRO

How to Command the Business Stage and

Dramatically Increase Your Sales With

Proven Acting Techniques

By Julie Hansen

THE CAREER PRESS, INC.
Pompton Plains, NJ

Copyright © 2011 by Julie Hansen

ACT LIKE A SALES PRO
EDITED AND TYPESET BY NICOLE DEFELICE
Cover design by Wes Youssi
Printed in the U.S.A.

To order this title, please call toll-free 1-800-CAREER-1 (NJ and Canada: 201-848-0310) to order using VISA or MasterCard, or for further information on books from Career Press.

The Career Press, Inc.
220 West Parkway, Unit 12
Pompton Plains, NJ 07444
www.careerpress.com

Library of Congress Cataloging-in-Publication Data
Hansen, Julie, 1961-
   How to command the business stage and dramatically increase your sales with proven acting techniques / by Julie Hansen.
      p. cm.
   Includes bibliographical references and index.
   ISBN 978-1-60163-167-1 -- ISBN 978-1-60163-659-1 (ebook)
      1. Selling. I. Title.

   HF5438.25.H356 2011
   658.85--dc22
                                                                2011003480

DEDICATION
&
ACKNOWLEDGMENTS

To my parents, Jean and Larry Hansen.

Like any great stage production, I've been fortunate enough to be a part of, there is an exceptional cast behind the scenes deserving of applause:

CAST (IN ORDER OF APPEARANCE)

Nathan Teegarden helped me connect the dots between acting and sales, encouraging me to aim high and helping me create a roadmap for getting there. Without him, I'm not sure this book would exist.

I thank my agent, Pat Snell, for believing this deserved to be a book and for providing patient guidance and experienced direction from concept to completed manuscript. The president of the Michael Snell Literary Agency, Michael Snell, came up with the perfect title.

Thanks to the folks at Career Press, especially Nicole DeFelice and Kirsten Dalley, who made the editing process much less painful than rumored.

I owe a great deal to my family. My father, Larry Hansen, serves as a daily inspiration and a powerful example of an authentic, passionate sales professional. My mother, Jean Hansen, was always there with strength, humor, and cake when the obstacles seemed daunting. My sister, Shelly Burnett, had an unwavering faith in me that often outshone my own and carried me through many early drafts. My brother, Dan Hansen, served up his experience as the consummate sales pro to a sister who once served him the consummate mud pie. My nephew, Matt Burnett, offered a discerning eye and fresh perspective.

Special thanks to Beau Lundy for encouraging me on this path. He deserves a standing ovation for tirelessly listening to my ideas and readily offering the perfect example or turn of a phrase.

Thank you to my talented friend Molly Gibson, who never refused a request for coffee or advise. Her remarkable faith, insight, and good sense kept me on track and helped shape many a chapter.

I was fortunate throughout this process to have a fine ensemble of friends who played a variety of supportive roles, especially: Ruth Freshman, Barbara Vonderheid, Amy St. Denis, Tricia Forbes, Becky Laschanzky, Jeanne Waller, Heather Lindemann, Roberta Cedillo, Bliss Holland, Terry Datz, and Chuck Lontine.

Thank you to sales pro, Mary Rawlins for reading an early draft. Louise Hodges, Richard Weekly, Louise Stephens, Marilyn Dana and Jed Esposito for contributing their stories.

A final round of applause for Dessie Fafoutis, Gary Moore, Barry Farber, and Diane Conway for so generously sharing their experience and wisdom, and Nicole Lombard and Andrew Honey at *ThinkSales Magazine*, Bart Taylor, and Mike Cote and company at *ColoradoBiz* for championing my work.

And now…curtains up.

CONTENTS

INTRODUCTION:
THE NATURAL

"I feel I have to work hard to nurture whatever talent I have as an actor. I feel like it's not natural to me. So I don't take it for granted…"

~David Duchovny

In the early 1980s, I was a rookie selling air-time on a Top 40 radio station to potential advertisers. I would spend hours preparing to make cold calls, then in a panic quickly hang up as soon as someone answered the phone. Thankfully, this was before Caller I.D. My presentations were hit or miss. Sometimes I would feel confident and animated, other times awkward and tongue-tied. The more pressure I felt to sell, the more inconsistent my performance. I envied those natural salespeople, the ones who always seemed to be on, the ones who took rejection in stride and continued to perform at their best. What was I lacking? Everyone said I was good with people, so what did these natural sellers have that I didn't, and how could I get my hands on it?

Despite dozens of training programs and vain attempts at emulating the style of my peers, I could never seem to get comfortable in my own skin. This led me to ask myself if I should find another career because I wasn't a natural. On the other hand, in what field was I a natural? I know now that if I had done only what came naturally to me, many of my best performances would never have happened. History is full of examples of those who have triumphed at something that seemed impossible, something that seemed to go against their natures: the Oprah Winfreys, the J.K. Rowlings, the Bill Porters (a salesman with cerebral palsy who inspired the movie *Door to Door*. See "Sales in the Movies" in the Appendix). How did they do it? By using that time-tested proverbial question and answer, "How do you get to Carnegie Hall? Practice, practice, practice." Perhaps of equal importance, they also practiced the right things.

I took my first acting class because I thought it would be fun. But I was also fearful. I thought I might be asked to do something embarrassing, such as crawl around on the floor like a snake or growl like a tiger. To my relief, I was asked to do neither. However, my relief was short-lived when I discovered that I was not a natural actor, either. Fortunately, not being a natural didn't stop me from having a good time and didn't prevent me from participating in the weekly exercises and scenes. I continued to practice at home because I discovered that the exercises had the added benefit of improving my focus and my ability to communicate effectively with clients. My teacher encouraged me to audition for plays and commercials, and much to my surprise, I would get cast. I eventually moved to New York City, where I went on to act in theater and national commercials, even winning a small role on HBO's *Sex and the City*, all while continuing to sell. I began to notice that the same skills I was using to win parts were helping me win more business. Soon I was breaking sales records, selling with confidence to Fortune 500 companies, and eventually leading a national sales team. For the first time, I felt like I fit in my own skin!

It wasn't until I found acting that my sales career blossomed and the question of whether or not I was a natural became moot. Just as I was perhaps not born to be in sales, I discovered that most of today's so-called natural actors were not "to the stage born." Often what is perceived as natural talent is the result of years of dedication and training. People who are great at what they do make it look natural.

Before Clint Eastwood and Burt Reynolds were famous, they attended an audition together at Universal Studios. The studio executive sent them both packing, telling Clint that he spoke too slowly and his Adam's apple stuck out. As the story goes, Clint turned to Burt and said, "At least I can act." Burt shot back, "Yeah, I can learn to act. But you're going to have a hell of a time getting rid of that Adam's apple."[1]

Acting taught me one of my most valuable sales lessons. Everything I needed to be a great seller I already had within me; it was just a matter of how to access it. A truly great performance—whether on the business stage or on the Broadway stage—comes from within you. Acting will provide the key.

What is it about acting that has produced such dramatic and lasting effects in my sales career whereas other, more traditional sales training programs failed? Acting is the ultimate form of persuasion and engagement. A great actor inspires us, and holds our attention, sometimes for up to three hours, sometimes for as little as 30 seconds. These are abilities we'd all like to possess as salespeople. Although many sales books make comparisons that stretch the imagination, such as selling is like baseball, poker, or dating, this book will sell you on the notion that selling is, in fact, like acting. In the groundbreaking book, *The Experience Economy: Work Is Theatre & Every Business a Stage*, Harvard MBAs Pine and Gilmore assert: "Selling, whether pitching automobiles or bottles of perfume, is theater."[2] Each day, we play dozens of roles, displaying enthusiasm we don't always feel, or speaking words we didn't write. If you think about it, we are all acting. Whether we're doing it well will be shown in the results.

Whereas acting has evolved a lot over the past century, sales has not. Modern acting is about working from the inside out—not the external, heavily stylized performances of the early 1900s. It's about trusting what you feel and connect to on the inside will be communicated on the outside, and that the truth is always more compelling than a false representation. Yet surprisingly, most sales books and training programs continue to focus almost exclusively on techniques that involve making external changes without altering what's happening on the inside, such as neuro-linguistic programming, mirroring, leading questions, and scripted delivery. As salespeople, it is time for us to evolve, because, let's face it, the old ways are not working anymore.

What follows is a compilation of proven acting techniques that have produced some of stage and screen's most influential stars, such as Marlon Brando, Robert DeNiro, Meryl Streep, Denzel Washington, and Angelina Jolie. I've adapted these techniques to fit each step of the sales model, from gaining the appointment to closing the deal—and everything in between. You won't be asked to quack like a duck or buzz like a bee; however, you will be challenged to step outside of your comfort zone. But if you're in sales, aren't you outside of your comfort zone almost every day? Acting, like sales, is about taking risks.

If you're looking for dramatic and lasting change in your ability to win sales, I encourage you to keep an open mind and put the principles in this book to work for you. A simple step-by-step format makes it easy for you to incorporate these new skills immediately, and the exercises at the end of each chapter and sales coaching scenes will help you find solutions to common issues among today's sellers. Each chapter will provide you with a new set of tools to help you discover that performer within, learn to flex new selling muscles, outsell the competition, and consistently deliver the sales performance of your life!

"I believe we all have two lives: the one we learn with, and the one we live after that."

~Glenn Close as Iris Gaines in *The Natural*

ACT I:
The Rehearsal

THE CASTING CALL: MAKING A FIRST IMPRESSION

1

"Actors ought to be larger than life. You come across quite enough ordinary, nondescript people in daily life and I don't see why you should be subjected to them on the stage too."

~Donald Sinden, British actor, Royal Shakespeare Company

Sheryl begins her sales pitch. As she reads from a PowerPoint slide, her voice is tentative, her delivery wooden, and her body language stiff. And it's all downhill from there. A crucial seven seconds has passed, and Sheryl is just now becoming more animated, adding gestures, finding her voice, and finally injecting personality into her presentation. But it's too late. She is past the point of no return and an important sale has slipped by. All in just seven seconds!

7 SECONDS

Experts say that we form a first impression in as little as seven seconds.[1] Most salespeople fail to make a memorable first impression. It's not that we're not interesting, charming, or talented; it's because we don't do anything to make ourselves stand out from the crowd. It is rare that a sales presentation is remembered with any type of clarity the next day, week, or month. I've seen more memorable performances take place *inside* the sales office when a seller recounts his drive into work to his coworkers! If salespeople are usually engaging, vibrant people, why does their sense of performance and individuality so often get checked at the door?

Make no mistake, salespeople must be every bit the performer an actor is in order to stand out in an increasingly crowded playing field. In today's economy, that winning trifecta of right product, right price, and right timing is no longer enough to ensure getting—or keeping—the business. Like a compelling actor that draws us in from the first scene, a successful salesperson must take command of the business stage at the outset. You do not need to learn to juggle, tell a joke, or pull a rabbit out of a hat. Early in Richard Burton's career, critics said he had "a trick for getting the maximum of attention with a minimum of fuss."[2] That's the kind of impression we should strive for as salespeople. We need to create a unique and memorable first impression in order to help our prospect distinguish us from the many other "ordinary, nondescript people" vying for his attention: maximum attention, minimum fuss.

ARE YOU MEMORABLE?

Clients generally like me. They remember me...most of the time...I think.

Are you brave enough to take the following quiz and find out just how memorable you are?

True or False:

1. I have no problem getting a new prospect on the phone or scheduling a follow-up meeting.

2. I receive a prompt response (within 24 hours) from my prospects when I make a follow-up call or send an e-mail.

3. I can sum up what I do in an interesting seven-second sound bite that engages my prospects and prompts them to ask questions.

4. I am introduced to others by clients, and they are able to enthusiastically and succinctly state what I do.

5. I receive the first phone call when a prospect I've previously met with is ready to buy.

If you didn't answer True to all five questions, you are, as they say, leaving money on the table. "But I'm no Richard Burton!" you say. True enough. Although this book will not teach you how to take command of the stage by playing Hamlet or King Arthur, it will show you how to take command of the sale—from the first step to the last, by mastering the Three Acts of Sales Showmanship.

THE THREE ACTS OF SALES SHOWMANSHIP

☆ Act 1: **Develop** a strong command of voice, mind, and body.

☆ Act 2: **Communicate** with intention and impact.

☆ Act 3: **Engage** consumers by creating memorable buying experiences.

Think of some of the most compelling actors of our time and you'll notice they have these three things in common:

1. A strong command of their voice and body, whether they speak impeccably (Morgan Freeman or Anthony Hopkins), with a stutter (Jimmy Stewart), or with an impediment (Marlee Matlin).

2. A clear and persuasive communication of their intentions (Sandra Bullock in *The Blind Side*, Daniel Day-Lewis in *There Will Be Blood*, Susan Sarandon in *Dead Man Walking*).

3. A memorable performance that draws us in (Tom Hanks in *Philadelphia*, Meryl Streep in *The Devil Wears Prada*, Jeff Bridges in *Crazy Heart*).

We remember these fine actors and listen and watch with rapt attention, no matter what role they're playing. They have risen to the top of their industry through a dedication to their craft and a keen sense of showmanship. By adding the Three Acts of Sales Showmanship to each stage of the sales process—from getting the appointment to following up after the sale—you can create a memorable buying experience and rise to the top of your industry.

So where do you begin? Typically, the first gatekeeper an actor encounters on the road to success is a casting director. In sales, it is your prospect.

Your Prospect, the Casting Director

Professional casting directors are experts at quickly spotting talent. They have to be, because they may see up to a thousand actors for one role. They typically allot a very small amount of time for each actor—as much as 30 minutes or as little as 30 seconds. All day, a steady parade of actors auditioning for the same role, repeating the same lines over and over, stretches out ahead of them, until suddenly, someone enters the room who is somehow different from the rest, commanding the casting directors' attention with a powerful presence, interesting actions, and a compelling delivery. Though the actor is reading from the same script, it is as if the casting directors are hearing the words for the very first time. They give that actor more time than all of the others auditioning. They coach him to get just the right performance for the camera. Every actor who auditioned prior is pushed out of their minds—and everyone who comes after has a higher bar to reach. Casting directors and prospects alike are waiting for that one person to wow them, wake them up, and make their decision easy.

If your prospect sees a fair number of salespeople (and he probably does), he is, in his own right, an expert at spotting sales talent. Put yourself in his shoes: Each day, one salesperson after another comes in hawking their wares: We're the best…blah, blah, blah…Buy my product, blah, blah, blah. We all blur together after a while. Sellers are often shielded from their competition and that makes it easier to forget about them. Sure, you may sit next to a competitor in the waiting room once in a while, but you don't know how many sales calls or appointments your prospect takes during the course of a week. As an actor, more often than not, I was thrust face-to-face with my competition. I've been sent on cattle calls where the room is full of a hundred actors, all just slightly different versions of me: taller, rounder, younger, older, blonder. When you're face-to-face with a hundred actors competing for one part, the need to stand out suddenly becomes very clear.

Today's businesspeople, like casting directors, have a very limited amount of time and hundreds of people competing for it, which means you need to grab their attention immediately and hang on. Just as an actor needs to quickly demonstrate why he's right for the part and deserves to be heard, you need to convince your prospects that you are right for their business.

Let's see what casting directors say makes an actor quickly stand out and relate that to how we can make a strong first impression with our prospects.

THE 12 BE'S FOR A MEMORABLE FIRST IMPRESSION

Be prepared.

Smart actors find out as much about the role before the audition as they can. When you're meeting with someone for the first time, learn as much about her and her company as possible. If you're stretched for time, a quick scan of the company's Website and About Us section will give you enough information to speak intelligently. According to a former client who buys media for a large advertising agency, nothing is more irritating than having to explain his business or industry to a new salesperson when that information is readily available elsewhere. Questions, casting directors say, should not be used to teach you their business. They primarily should be used to help you gain clarity and make connections between what they do and you do. Use your audition time wisely: connect, make an impression and create interest. (More in Chapter 3.)

Be personable.

You're a person first—a businessperson second. "People don't hire actors. They hire people who can act," says casting director Peter Kelley. "When it's close—and it often is—sometimes hiring decisions have to do with the person as much as the performance."[3] The same applies to salespeople. Don't hide behind your product or service or rely on it to speak for itself. Let your personality shine through and show your uniqueness, if only in some small way. Make it easy for people to get to know you. (More in Chapter 8.)

Be interesting.

Seems simple, right? Yet, you can't imagine how many people come in and say the same mundane things, according to one well-known casting director. The person on the other side of the desk is looking for something that will set you apart, but most people give him very little to work with. Think about when you meet someone for the first time. Aren't you secretly hoping he'll say something interesting, such as "I'm an astronaut," or "I'm on the Canadian luge team"? I'm not suggesting you lie, but you can certainly pick out the most interesting aspects of who you are or what you do, and weave them into your introduction or answer to common questions such as "What do you do? How long have you been with XYZ Company?" Focus on your uniqueness in order to differentiate yourself and be remembered. (More in Chapter 7.)

Be attentive.

Really listen—don't just pretend. You're not fooling anyone; we all know when someone is listening to us or not. The camera and the human eye can pick up the truth. Don't mentally check out or speak when it's not your turn. And don't be afraid to pause and let what the other person said sink in. President of New York's Creative Talent Company, Breanna Benjamin, says that casting directors like to see an actor think and respond thoughtfully.[4] And what client wouldn't like to see that you're taking in what he has to say and processing it before just blurting out your next line? (More in Chapter 10.)

Be bold.

Salespeople, like actors, often make the mistake of holding back until they've gauged the temperature of the other person or the room before committing and going all in. Actors should never assume they'll get another take and salespeople should never assume they will get a second chance. Remember the seven-second rule and don't be tentative. Take a risk and blow them away the first time. Don't rely on the prospect or client to ask you just the right question or pull the information out of you. Be ready to jump in by using whatever opportunity presents itself—or create your own. (More in Chapter 9.)

Be focused.

You want to connect with the person you're talking to and exude confidence and trustworthiness. Nothing says lack of confidence or unreliability like poor eye contact. Most of us know better than to look over someone's shoulder while in the midst of a conversation, but maintaining constant eye contact can be just as off-putting. Those of us trained in neuro-linguistic programming, mirroring, and the like, often come away with the idea that the more eye contact the better. Frankly, laser-like eye contact is simply unnatural and borders on creepy. It's natural to glance away while thinking or processing information and it gives the other person some much appreciated space. (More in Chapter 8.)

Be committed.

When an actor abruptly drops a line or his character before the camera has gotten the full take, the entire shot is ruined. Any good work he's done prior to that moment is useless. In the same way, don't cut yourself off too soon. Don't blow mistakes out of proportion and draw unnecessary attention to them. Though you want to be aware of your prospect's reactions, don't let every little sound or movement distract you and bring you to a halt. On the other hand, don't be afraid to pause after making a point. Hold your last beat; let the impact of what you said stick before moving on. (More in Chapter 11.)

Be confident.

Believe you have something of value to offer. Believe you are someone worthy of the investment in a conversation. If you don't believe it, others won't either. Casting directors want to believe that the next actor through the door is going to be the answer to their dreams. No matter how prickly some prospects are, they want to believe you can help them solve their problems. Don't dissuade them from that notion by apologizing for taking up their time or excessively thanking them for giving you their time. After all, isn't making good, sound choices part of their job? You can be courteous without showing a lack of confidence. (More in Chapter 12.)

Be in the moment.

When you meet someone, you never know whether you'll have 30 seconds or 30 minutes, so always be prepared for different periods of time. Be prepared with a one-minute brief introduction, five-minute mini-pitch, 15-minute semi-pitch, and 30-minute full presentation. Be ready to adjust on the fly. If you are truly "in the moment," you are prepared, really listening, and reading your prospect's body language. You will have made the most out of each encounter no matter how brief, and you will not have overstayed your welcome. (More in Chapter 13.)

Be professional.

Along with being prepared, this seems obvious, yet it comes up repeatedly with casting directors and clients, and is therefore worth mentioning. What does being professional mean?

Be early.

Being on time just makes you average. Not only does being early show respect, but it allows you to get acquainted with the room, do any last-minute preparations, and regain precious focus that you may have lost riding up the elevator with the cast from *Jersey Shore*. I've had enough nail-biting experiences missing a freeway exit or arriving at the wrong campus of a large multi-national company to realize that being early is the goal, not a fortunate coincidence of Mapquest and traffic gods.

Be nice.

The receptionist could be your client's best friend. The client may be the guy on whom you closed the elevator door. No matter what happens (the client takes a phone call or walks out of the room) always assume you are being watched—from the moment you pull into the parking garage until you are waving goodbye in your rearview mirror. I once auditioned for a casting director who was simultaneously eating a sandwich and texting someone on her BlackBerry. Though I wondered why I should bother continuing with the audition, I kept going. Much to my surprise, I got the part. (More in Chapter 10.)

Be clear.

Do you want an appointment, an order—not sure? Whatever it is, you can be assured it will come across whether you verbalize it or not. It is easy for both actors and sellers to lose sight of what they're there for, especially after sitting in a crowded waiting room for an hour with a dozen competitors. The temptation to socialize or flip through a magazine to relieve the pressure can be overwhelming—and deadly. Be clear and specific about what you want before you arrive, and don't let anything keep you from doggedly pursuing your goal until you leave. (More in Chapter 5.)

Be flexible.

Casting directors love an actor who can take direction—just as your customers do. Does this mean you should throw your whole presentation out the window if their suggestions are vastly different from what you had in mind? No. Instead, try to incorporate what they say into your presentation. It shows that you're flexible and you're listening and responding, rather than remaining solely focused on forcing your own agenda. (More in Chapter 13.)

The next time you leave a prospect's office, ask yourself the same questions an actor asks himself after an audition: "Did I master the Three Acts of Showmanship? Did I show a strong command of my voice and body? Did I communicate my intentions clearly and persuasively? Did I draw them in and engage them? Did I give them a reason to remember me?"

The following chapters are dedicated to helping you consistently answer those questions with a resounding yes!

THE ROLE:
THROW OUT THE ONE-SIZE-
FITS-ALL SALES HAT

2

"With any part you play, there is a certain amount of yourself in it. There has to be, otherwise it's just not acting. It's lying."

~Johnny Depp

Everything Terry was taught about sales reinforced the idea that he had to be "larger than life," or someone other than he was, in order to be successful. Each day, Terry would put on his "sales hat"—you know the one: loud, over-the-top, and ill-fitting. Almost instantaneously, the normally soft-spoken, sincere Terry would disappear, replaced by a two-dimensional sales stereotype. Although Terry had occasional successes, he felt like a phony, and even his clients could sense an incongruity between himself and his message, and a lack of real connection to his product.

By exploring roles from his own life, such as that of student and coach, and applying them to his sales career, Terry was able to find his own unique sales style. He soon gained enough confidence to hang up the one-size-fits-all sales hat for good, and is now admired and trusted by hundreds of clients and is at the top of his game in his industry.

Like Terry, you don't have to put on a role in order to be effective. By using the simple tools outlined in this chapter, you will learn how to put yourself *into* your role, a rewarding journey that will lead to greater sales success, increased confidence, and a welcome comfort in your own skin— whether presenting one-on-one or to large groups.

In this chapter, you will learn a simple, step-by-step process for developing your own unique role as a salesperson.

Acting techniques for creating your unique sales role:

☆ Throw away the sales hat.

☆ Define the seven roles in the sales process.

☆ Learn the five steps to developing your role.

☆ Harness the qualities of a sales pro.

YOUR ROLE VS. ROLE-PLAYING

Don't confuse your sales role with role-playing, which will be discussed in greater detail in Chapter 8. Role-playing sends most sellers running for the nearest exit, mumbling something about a "really important meeting." Your hesitation is justified. Role-playing typically involves you and one of your colleagues in the hot seat as your manager eagerly anticipates your demonstration of "how we tow the company line." Your peers sit back and snicker, grateful to have dodged the bullet—this time. Summoning up all of your acting ability, you proceed to put on the role that you think is expected of you, the role of what you imagine a really super-salesperson might be like, if he or she in fact existed—a role that has little or no resemblance to *you* on an actual sales call.

"Roles are phony!"

No wonder you think roles are phony! But there's a big difference between putting on a role and *assuming* a role, which is what this chapter is about. You're actually assuming a role right now. Perhaps you are in your student role as you read this, but later you may be a mother, a husband, a cook, or a yoga instructor. We play dozens of different roles every day. We don't turn into an entirely different person, but we bring different facets of our personalities to the role while leaving out other, less appropriate parts. We don't talk to our managers the way we do our children, and we don't talk to our clients the way we do our mothers (hopefully!). The personality traits you exhibit in these roles make up the complex creature you are, and they vary depending upon your relationships, your circumstances, and your objectives.

Think about your own sales role for a moment. Does it fit? Are you perhaps a little uncomfortable, like Terry, a bit at odds with who you really are? Are you trying to be someone you're not, someone more interesting or assertive? Odds are that, like most people, you're doing it unconsciously, haphazardly, with inconsistent and unreliable results. As salespeople, too often we don't know what works or doesn't work or why. We just forge ahead putting out more calls, making more presentations, doing more, more, more—on the theory that the odds will eventually work in our favor. Maybe they will, but imagine if you could fine-tune that process and know precisely why something worked, effortlessly recreating it each time. Acting provides a method for creating the best possible role for any situation using your own personality and experience. Because really, what else do you have to work with?

Actors can re-create powerful performances night after night during a Broadway show or day after day on a movie set with countless stops and starts precisely because they have a technique. Little is left to chance, though you would think otherwise by watching. When actors give truly great performances, we are apt to say "Wow! They didn't even look like they were acting!" The same can be said for great salespeople. They don't even look like they're selling. So how can you get to that place?

Create your own unique sales role.

During the filming of *My Left Foot*, Daniel Day-Lewis, who played a severely handicapped character, refused to break character off-screen, insisting that he be lifted in and out of his wheelchair and wheeling himself around the set in order to gain insight into his character's life.[1] The result was an Academy Award and two broken ribs from assuming a painful, hunched-over position for weeks at a time.

To prepare for a scene in *Marathon Man,* Dustin Hoffman went for several days without sleep, showering, or shaving. He was looking pretty rough when fellow actor Laurence Olivier asked him why he was putting himself through such an ordeal. Hoffman answered that he was trying to be convincing in the role. Olivier replied, "Dear boy, it's called *acting.*"[2]

There are as many ways to get into a role as there are schools of acting, including the rather extreme measures previously described. Fortunately, there is no need for you to forego a shower or sleep, or sit hunched over in a wheelchair all day. Most of the characteristics that define a successful salesperson are already within you just waiting to be coaxed out and directed.

"The basic components of the characters we will play are somewhere within ourselves." ~Uta Hagen, actress and author of *A Challenge for the Actor*

Throw away the sales hat.

Before we can create our ideal sales role, we must first throw away the idea that there is one personality type into which you must squeeze yourself. There is no super-seller persona that you can simply assume. You can not automatically be like your cubicle mate who starts every presentation with a joke, or your manager who speaks in all caps and exclamation points. You alone must find your style. You could stumble around and experiment for years, *or* you could try the route that thousands of actors have used to find their way into a role.

Who am I?

When taking on a role in a play, film, or television show, the actor's first step is to analyze the character, looking for shared experiences, feelings, behavior, or circumstances in order to personally relate to the role and ultimately deliver a "real" and convincing performance.

As actors do, in order to fit ourselves to the sales role, we must first establish what that role requires, what common qualities and characteristics we share, and determine how we're going to bring those characteristics out.

In most areas of our life, this process takes place unconsciously; we simply bring the role best-suited to each situation and relationship. When we are shopping for a car, we are consumers looking for reliable information and assistance. However, if we run into someone we know, we suddenly shift into our role as friend or neighbor. But imagine for a moment the havoc that would ensue if we mixed up our roles—playing confidante to the president of our company or practical joker to our most important client. Consciously choosing which role we are going to assume and what that means in terms of behavior ensures that the best and most appropriate "you" is present for each situation. After all, you don't want the "you" that's sitting on the couch with the dog and channel surfing to show up for a big sales presentation, do you?

ROLES WITHIN THE SALES PROCESS

There are seven basic roles most salespeople must play at some point within the sales process, regardless of the type of product or service being sold. These include:

1. The Cold-Caller: Contacts potential customers and creates sufficient curiosity or interest in the product/service to get an appointment or make a sale.

2. The Interviewer: Asks guided questions to discover buyer needs and objections in order to determine best possible solutions and create a game plan.

3. The Presenter: Showcases, demonstrates, or reveals the product/service in its best possible light to generate interest.

4. The Entertainer: Engages prospects and/or clients by developing rapport and a relationship.

5. The Negotiator: Facilitates arriving at best possible solutions for both parties.

6. The Persuader: Motivates clients to purchase product/service through compelling stories, examples, or evidence.

7. The Closer: Asks for the sale clearly and consistently.

Most salespeople are uncomfortable with at least one—if not more—of these roles, whether it's getting the appointment, handling objections, or asking for the sale. This discomfort can lead to a variety of compensating behaviors, such as avoiding making phone calls (when you hate cold calling), talking too much (when you don't like handling objections), readily agreeing with everything the client says (when you're afraid of conflict), or simply not asking for the sale.

Obviously, if we are not performing to full capacity in each of the seven roles of the sales process, we are limiting our potential to walk out the door with a sale. The following five-step process ensures that we are performing each role to the best of our ability.

5 STEPS TO ROLE DEVELOPMENT

1. Identify your weak or uncomfortable roles within the sales process (such as closing).

2. Examine compensating behaviors you use to deal with that discomfort (such as avoiding asking for the sale).

3. Determine which qualities would address your fears or discomfort.

4. Discover where you exhibit these qualities in other roles in your life (such as the *tenaciousness* we exhibit when learning to master a new skill).

5. Decide how you would apply qualities from this role to your sales role.

Let's look at each step more closely.

1. Identify weak or uncomfortable roles.

Friendly and outgoing, Lisa freezes up whenever she gets in front of more than one person to pitch her creative services. Naturally gregarious and knowledgeable about his product, Joel gets nervous and tongue-tied when it comes time to ask for the sale. So whereas Lisa struggles with the role of the presenter, Joel's challenge comes during his role as the closer.

Closing, presenting, entertaining, cold-calling, negotiating—depending upon your personality type, any or all of these can cause stress during the sales process. There may also be additional roles unique to your industry or product that you struggle with as well. Whatever they are, when called upon to perform them, we may experience feelings of anxiousness, inadequacy, or uncertainty.

Identifying and giving a name to the roles that produce negative feelings starts to shed some light on our fears and self-defeating behaviors, opening the door to a process that will take us from panic to performance.

2. Examine compensating behaviors.

When uncomfortable with a particular role, we may unconsciously fall back on behaviors that make us comfortable—even though they may sabotage our progress. Following is a list of common forms of compensating behaviors we may use within the sales process to our detriment. See if you recognize yourself in any of them.

The Cold-Caller

Cold-calling is one of the most disliked and heavily debated roles within sales, and the simplest form of compensating is to avoid making the calls. Perhaps we make the calls, but we do it with a great sense of dread, anticipating rejection or assuming a lack of interest or need. Maybe we only call people we know will give us positive feedback, even though they provide nothing in the way of new business opportunities.

Add the pressure of a manager asking you to substantiate a minimum number of cold calls each day or week (as they often do), and you may find yourself exaggerating or even lying about the number of calls you're making, which adds a whole new layer of pressure and discomfort.

The Interviewer

Asking the hard questions is the best way to determine what the client's needs are, if we are able to address them, and how. Many sellers are excellent talkers, but poor listeners. This combination can result in asking questions without really "hearing" the answers, which is critical in order to adjust future questions and/or the direction of the call. Some sellers don't ask questions at all and assume everyone is in agreement if nothing is said. They may fear opening the door to potential conflict or being unable to answer a question put to them. Whatever the reason, a lot of important information is left locked up inside our prospect and we end up expending our precious energy and time doing guesswork.

The Presenter

Presenting a product or service to an individual customer or a group can bring on stage fright—regardless of the lack of a stage. This topic is discussed in detail in Chapter 12; however, fear of presenting can manifest itself in the following ways: avoiding group meetings or meetings with higher-level executives, under- or over-preparing, or focusing more on the act of presenting than communicating the message. End result: a weak or ineffective presentation and a lost opportunity to make a compelling case for your product or service.

The Entertainer

Few of us are professional comedians or talk show hosts, and holding ourselves up to those standards can keep us from trying to create a natural rapport. This common fear of being able to sustain someone's interest or be entertaining *enough* can lead us to avoid opportunities to connect with our clients outside of the normal business arena, such as meals or industry events where important bonding can take place. We may "forget" to keep in touch with clients when there's no deal pending to avoid engaging in that torture known as small talk. Avoiding personal interaction with our clients puts us at risk for losing any connection we may have painstakingly established, or dropping off their radar entirely.

The Negotiator

Most people hate conflict and sellers are no different in this regard. Fear of conflict in sales can manifest itself in changing the subject at the first sign of a disagreement, creating a distraction or jumping at the first solution offered—even if it is not the desired outcome or in everyone's best interests.

The Persuader

The ability to gracefully lead a buyer toward a decision without being too forceful or too subtle is a huge challenge for many sellers. If we're too pushy, we risk turning them off entirely; if we're too tentative, we risk not selling them on our product or service, often shutting down our pitch too early when the water appears to be getting a little rough. Either way, we've made the next role even harder for ourselves.

The Closer

When it comes to the most anxiety-producing role in sales, it's undoubtedly a tie between the closer and the cold-caller. Both involve being assertive, being persistent, and fearlessly throwing ourselves into unknown territory. When we are uncomfortable closing, we are often vague about our goals or intentions. We may go into a call with a general hope and wish that things will naturally lead to a close, assuming that closing has more to do with fate and the fickle mood of our client than anything else. But even fate—and your client—need a nudge sometimes, which must come from you.

In an effort to avoid the unsavory task of asking someone to buy something and possibly being told no, I've seen salespeople do all kinds of self-defeating dances: suggesting unnecessary additional steps, offering to return with irrelevant information, recommending the client confer with others, offering to set future appointments, waiting until the weather changes—even talking a client out of making a decision. All of these amount to prolonging the sales process and putting off the inevitable. Just like asking out that hot guy or girl, many of us subconsciously would rather hope there's a chance than hear a definitive no and have that doubt removed.

3. Determine qualities that would produce more positive results.

There are a number of studies done on what traits are shared by successful salespeople. I've broken down what I consider to be the top 25 qualities of successful salespeople:

☆ Assertive
☆ Committed
☆ Competent
☆ Competitive
☆ Confident
☆ Cooperative
☆ Courageous
☆ Creative
☆ Curious
☆ Disciplined
☆ Empathetic
☆ Energetic

☆ Flexible
☆ Focused
☆ Goal-oriented
☆ Likeable
☆ Passionate
☆ Persistent
☆ Positive
☆ Resilient
☆ Responsible
☆ Self-reliant
☆ Sincere
☆ Willing to learn

Though this list may seem overwhelming, look for the qualities in which you could use the most improvement. You may find that, although you are competent and creative, you are lacking in focus or persistence. Perhaps you are empathetic and passionate, but need more confidence. The following steps will help you discover and develop these traits to achieve peak performance.

4. Discover where we exhibit these qualities in other roles.

Look closely at the previous list. You probably embody most of these qualities in some area of your life. How can you access them to serve you in the sales process?

Consider the quality of assertiveness, which *Dictionary.com* defines as: confidently aggressive, self-assured; positive; forceful, decisive, forward. In what part of the sales process would this be most effective? Probably any, but assertiveness would definitely be helpful when it comes to cold-calling, negotiating, and closing.

Where in your life are you confidently aggressive or self-assured? How about forceful and decisive?

Assertiveness

Margot knew she was not assertive enough in sales calls and that it was costing her business. Instead of confronting it, she would shy away from cold-calling and fidget through a closing, backing off at the slightest hint of resistance. Walking through the previously outlined steps, she realized that she had very recently exhibited assertiveness while serving on the board of her home-owner's association. When brought to her attention that the elevators in her building were in need of serious repair, she promptly took charge, relaying her concerns to the management company in a straightforward, solutions-oriented manner. When her requests were ignored, Margot organized a committee to rally the owners to put pressure on the company. Margot's efforts resulted in new elevators for the building—without a special assessment to any of the residents. With this newly discovered assertiveness, Margo was able to close a prospect who had been putting her off for months by asking probing questions and presenting sound reasons to move forward with the sale.

5. Decide how to apply this quality to your sales role.

Realizing you already have the desired quality within you should come as something of a relief. Now how do you channel that quality into your sales role? It's easier than you think. Consider the following example.

<u>PERSISTENCE: A SALES PRO SCENE</u>

THE CAST

LEE: A pharmaceutical sales rep for a new ADHD (attention deficit hyperactivity disorder) drug.

DR. M.: A pediatrician with a large and successful practice.

THE SETTING

Lee works for a pharmaceutical company selling a fairly new ADHD drug to pediatricians and child psychiatrists. He is having difficulty getting the doctors to prescribe his product because as the third brand to market in its class, his drug is not significantly different from the market leader other than in the reduction of certain side effects. It's simply easier for the doctors not to change prescriptions. Lee feels intimidated and guilty asking doctors to take more time from their already-busy schedules to learn why they should prescribe his drug, so he backs off at the first sign of rejection.

DIRECTOR'S SCENE NOTES:

JH

Looking at your situation objectively—without judgment—what quality would keep you from being put off by these doctors so easily?

LEE

I guess persistence.

JH

Let's see how Google defines persistence: To persevere in spite of opposition, obstacles, and discouragement, or to constantly repeat or continue. Based on that, where have you been the most persistent in your life?

LEE

It would have to be with my children.

JH

Give me a specific example.

LEE

Well, my youngest child has special needs and the school in our district didn't have a very good program for him, but the school outside of our district had a great one. Naturally, we wanted the best for our son, so we tried to enroll him in the one outside of our district, but we ran into all sorts of roadblocks.

JH

How did you handle that?

LEE

I just kept looking for ways around them. When the school officials said we couldn't get him into the new school because we were outside of the boundaries, I took it to the board of education. When they sat on it for a month, I got a thousand people to sign a petition and took it to a city council meeting. A representative there happened to have a special needs child as well, and he finally paved the way to get my son into the school he needed. Now he's doing very well.

JH

How did you keep fighting even when it was not looking promising? What kept you going?

LEE

I didn't think it was fair that my child's education should suffer just because we happened to live on the wrong side of a street. I knew there had to be a way to make it happen because it was the right thing to do—not just for my son, but for everyone in the community. All of our children should have the best possible education available so they can become contributing members of society. I kept carrying that message to everyone I met, and if they wouldn't listen or didn't get it, I found someone within their organization who did.

JH

So what can you take from that example of persistence and use in your current situation selling to Dr. M. and other busy physicians?

LEE

I could focus on the fact that prescribing my drug when it's indicated is in everyone's best interests: the doctors, because any time a patient is happy, this funnels up to them and if they are part of a managed care system, the doctors are being evaluated on quality of care; the nurses, because the drug produces less side effects, therefore they receive fewer callbacks about problems with the drug, so their time is spent more efficiently; and of course the patients. Parents should have an opportunity to hear about a new product that might better address their child's needs.

JH

And isn't that what we trust our doctors to do? To stay up to speed on new products so they can make the most informed choices?

LEE

Absolutely. Everyone deserves to have a choice.

JH

Do you see that your lack of persistence in pursuing an appointment with Dr. M. is about avoiding your own personal discomfort at the expense of helping potential patients?

LEE

I never thought of it that way before, but you're right. Sort of selfish, I guess!

JH

How might you exhibit the same persistence you showed in your son's case with Dr. M.?

LEE

First, I'd remind myself that my feelings are not important here; doing the right thing for the children who can benefit from our drug is what's important. I'd also go in with the mindset that seeing me is just as necessary as any of his other meetings with pharmaceutical reps and keep pursuing an appointment.

JH

And if he still won't hear you out?

LEE

I could get the attention of the head nurse and let her know specifically what type of patient my drug can benefit and the other physicians who are prescribing it. I could invite Dr. M. to a lunch to hear the opinion of one of his peers.

JH

Good. Everyone should get to make an informed choice.

EXERCISES

1. List five different roles you play within a week.

2. Identify which role in the sales process causes you the most discomfort.

3. Name two compensating behaviors you currently use to avoid this role or make it more comfortable.

4. Identify what quality you would need to exhibit to be more effective in this role.

5. Give an example of a role in another area of your life where you have demonstrated this quality.

6. Describe in detail how you would bring the desired quality from that role to your sales role.

THE AUDITION:
GETTING THE APPOINTMENT

3

"So here I am at my age, still auditioning."

~Geraldine Page, age 85

Carol sells on-line advertising for an entertainment network in Manhattan. She is expected to make seven face-to-face sales calls each day, competing with hundreds of other sales reps for the time and business of the same small core group of buyers. The competition is steep, but Carol has a winning formula. Before picking up the phone, she imagines receiving amazing news she can't wait to share, visualizes a positive reception from the buyer, and creates a suspenseful hook that provides only enough key information to leave the buyer wanting more. She books more appointments than anyone on her team and has been the top seller for two years running.

Most actors must audition for every role they get (unless they are Meryl Streep or Denzel Washington). Unless you are Tony Robbins or Jeffrey Gitomer, you will probably need to get a face-to-face appointment before you have an opportunity to sell your product or service. Given its obvious importance in the sales process, you'd think that as much attention would be given to *getting* the appointment as the actual sales call, but this is rarely the case in most companies.

Actors spend hours, days, sometimes weeks preparing for an audition that may last only 30 seconds. If they don't nail the audition, their chances of getting the part are zero. The same thing applies to sales. Get the appointment, and you have a chance at getting the sale. Don't, and it's on to the next lead (you do have an endless supply, right?). A small investment of time and energy in applying the following three acting techniques can dramatically increase your ability to get in front of decision-makers.

Acting techniques for getting the appointment:

☆ Creating a "Moment Before" that will energize and focus your call.

☆ Identifying and adjusting expectations.

☆ Adding suspense to book more appointments.

DIALING FOR DOLLARS

Dan, a seller of medical supplies, is dragging after a poor night's sleep due to an argument with his wife. Arriving at his desk, he immediately spills a $4 latte on his new pants and finds a message from his manager reminding him that he needs to have five qualified appointments set up by noon in order to meet his monthly goal. If you were in Dan's position, you would probably immediately jump in and start frantically dialing for dollars, right? Haven't we all been on both sides of that desperate phone call? The pressure is palpable. Rather than increasing the chance of a positive outcome, it often does just the opposite. There is a more effective strategy that will have Dan coming from a place of strength, confidence, and excitement. Sounds good, but how is that possible, given his current circumstances?

THE "MOMENT BEFORE"

When does your sales call begin? When you pick up the phone? When your prospect answers the phone? How about when you introduce yourself? It may surprise you to know that your sales call begins well before that first phone call or meeting. Professional actors know that their character's life does not begin when the curtain rises or the director shouts "Action!" The actor's character has been somewhere, done something, and had thoughts that influence her attitude, how she enters the room, and how she relates to her scene partner. In his book, *Audition,* Michael Shurtleff calls the preceding events the "Moment Before." In order to truthfully fulfill the requirements of the scene, the actor must select an imaginary experience—or "Moment Before"—prior to her entrance that will provide her with the necessary momentum to jump into a scene already in progress. This is especially important in film where scenes are regularly shot out of sequence and an actor has to achieve a big emotional moment on cue or when the scene begins in the middle of the action. A good example is Shakespeare's *Hamlet,* which opens with a sentinel asking "Who's there?" with a great sense of fear and foreboding. If the actor playing the sentinel has not made real for himself the existing preconditions that inspire this question—that is, a quiet nighttime watch interrupted by strange noises, or visions made eerier by the recent death of the king—the opening will fail to engage the audience and convey the sense of uncertainty and doom critical to establishing the tone of the play.

Just like the actor's character, we are all coming and going somewhere, and it affects the way we think, feel, and act. By selecting and focusing on the right "Moment Before" for our sales call, we can achieve an optimal state of being despite the unpredictability of life.

Business baggage

No one arrives anywhere without carrying some of the past with them. In relationships, we call this baggage. In business, I call this business baggage. Sometimes, as in Dan's example, the immediately preceding circumstances seem to conspire against us as everything goes wrong at the most inopportune times: We wake up a with a headache the morning of our big presentation. We get a call from the school nurse right before negotiating an annual contract. Although sometimes luck will fall in our favor, try as we might, we cannot always control external circumstances to bend to our needs. But we *can* exercise some control over our internal circumstances. By placing the focus on a "Moment Before" that inspires us and rouses us to action, we can ensure our entrances are always dynamic, upbeat, and appropriate for the situation. Consider the following two examples:

1. You have just come from a very sad movie. The dog died, the cat died, even the hamster met an untimely end. Wiping away a tear as you exit the lobby, you come face-to-face with a potential new client. You quickly try and pull yourself together, but even so your handshake is weak, your voice choked, and your enthusiasm dampened.

2. Now, imagine you just came from an inspirational movie. They thought he would never walk again, but he won the Boston marathon! She never had any schooling, but ended up ruling a small European country! Now, suppose you run into this same client. Your handshake is firm, your voice, strong, and you are brimming with goodwill for all of humanity. You've come from the same place, yet your client has formed quite a different impression of you, entirely based on your preceding mental and emotional experience.

How to create the ideal "Moment Before"

If the "Moment Before" is where your sales call begins, how do you find one that works for you? You can start by answering the following simple questions:

1. What emotions and/or state of being do you want to project?

2. What immediately preceding circumstances would lead you to feel this way?

3. Where would you be coming from, physically and emotionally?

4. What do your current circumstances have in common with your ideal "Moment Before"?

5. What image or object would help ground your "Moment Before" in reality (a photo of your child, an award you won, a pen you used to sign your big deal, and so on)?

Using Dan's example, lets see how his morning might go if, instead of desperate-dialing, he used a positive "Moment Before" in the same situation. Instead of reflexively grabbing the phone, Dan would get quiet and take a few minutes to focus on what attitude he wants to project—upbeat and confident. He would then determine what would bring about this change in attitude. Dan decides that receiving a phone call from a grateful client would do the job. Taking this a step further, Dan imagines a particular client's voice and how the conversation would take place. As his current circumstances would be the same as his imaginary circumstances (sitting at his desk), it is easy for Dan to physically ground himself in the "reality" of his new "Moment Before" by picking up the phone and imagining hearing his client tell him what a difference his product has made in the life of one of his patients. Dan then hangs up the phone after the "conversation" is over, and riding on the momentum he has just created, he picks it up again to make his first *real* sales call. His enthusiasm and desire to share this experience with a new client shines through the phone, and he easily lands the appointment.

Finding the right "Moment Before"

How do you find a "Moment Before" that gives you the same kind of momentum as Dan's did? What if your "Moment Before" doesn't work? Finding the right one for you may require some experimentation. Often, the things we think are going to inspire us don't translate into real feelings. You need to find something that moves you—and it may not be the first thing that comes to mind.

I once played the role of a woman whose husband left her for another man. In the scene, I was confronted with his infidelity for the first time and, of course, devastated by the news. It seemed natural that, prior to my entrance, I should focus on something very upsetting—an angry conversation, a betrayal—so that those feelings would be ready to come out at the right time. However, once on stage, I was surprised that I felt nothing. During rehearsals, I explored the character and myself a little deeper; I realized that my reaction would only be one of shock if, at the moment I found out, I was madly in love with my husband and under the assumption that things were wonderful between us. By placing my focus on all of the things I loved about him and the future I had looked forward to spending with him, I was able to experience something close to the shock and despair my character would feel at the revelation.

Finding a "Moment Before" that works for you is a personal journey. You may end up trying out several things before finding something that really moves you. You may discover that after a while your "Moment Before" has quit working for you and you need to find a new one. Whatever you do, don't give up until you find something that inspires you to the point where you can't wait to pick up that phone and make a call.

EXPECTATIONS

We never know what is going to happen next in life, but we almost always have expectations about it. Everything we do and say is based on our expectations. We turn the key in the ignition and expect the car to start. We wake up the baby and expect to hear a cry. We call our mothers and expect to hear how we never call our mothers. Are we surprised sometimes? Sure! Sometimes the car doesn't start, the baby doesn't cry, or our mothers don't make us feel guilty. But when we start out with expectations of how things will go, our actions tend to fall in line.

Imagine you are starting your car. It's been running fine and there's no reason to expect an exception on this particular day. So when you get into your car, you are thinking about where you are going to stop for coffee and making a mental note to pick up the dry cleaning. You put the key in the ignition, turn it, and quickly move on to adjusting your stereo and checking your rearview mirror as you back out of your parking space.

Now, imagine you are getting into your car after having had several problems with the starter. You sit at the wheel with a slight sense of dread, anticipating having to call AAA and wondering how long they will take to arrive, and just how late you are going to be for your meeting. You focus all of your attention on placing the key in the ignition "just right." You turn it, listening for that telltale *click* and perhaps looking to see if the engine light comes on. You breathe a sigh of relief as you make your way out of your parking garage, reminding yourself to get the starter checked before the warranty expires, and in the process, you completely forget about picking up the dry cleaning.

The car starts easily in both instances, but an entirely different set of behaviors results from our contrasting expectations.

Actors have a more challenging time with expectations than we do because they actually *do* know what's going to happen next in the script. In order to create realistic behavior, they must suspend their disbelief and knowledge of what is to come and try to live completely moment-to-moment in order to register surprise, anger, hurt, or whatever is called for in the scene. In sales, you don't know what's coming, so the expectations are absolutely yours to imagine. Why not make them work for you instead of against you?

Evaluate your expectations

Ask yourself what you expect to happen on this cold call, appointment, or presentation. Is it positive or negative? Be honest. How many of us make a phone call or walk into a business with a negative expectation about how we will be received: *They're going to be annoyed. They hate salespeople.* Or what the outcome will be: *They're happy with their current supplier. This is a waste of time.* We're defeated before we even get in the door! Anything that supports this expectation, such as an abrupt secretary, a gruff-sounding client, or even a busy signal, we use to support our case, often magnifying its significance. Maybe we get a client on the phone who sounds rushed and impatient. Many of us automatically assume we are interrupting something very important. In response, our tone turns apologetic, and we rush through our call, stumbling to an abrupt conclusion. Naturally, the client does have something more important to do than listen to our jumbled hyper-pitch. We are so quick to assume that the other person's state has something to do with us—when we have yet to even meet him or make a first impression!

What is the best-case scenario?

Instead of jumping to the negative, consider the best-case scenario: customers calling you so that you never have to prospect again? Let me know if you find that job! Let's try the *second* best-case scenario: You call a prospect and he shows interest in your product or service, has a need for it, and would like to get together with you to learn more about it. Would that be okay with you? If that is your expectation, even if the person sounds hurried or bothered, instead of taking it personally, you might assume that he is dealing with a heavy workload. Or maybe he just hung up with his attorney. Or he is in a very boring meeting and grateful for an excuse to get out of it.

Anticipate that each new prospect would be thrilled to hear how you can solve his problem, improve his business, become a valuable resource, or even become a potential new friend. How different is your tone, your attitude, and your behavior when you are talking to people who you believe are happy to hear from you and that you know you are going to help?

SUSPENSE

Salespeople make one common mistake when they are trying to get an appointment: They provide too much information. Yes, you need to identify yourself and explain why you're calling, but more often than not, salespeople turn this simple two-sentence process into a two-minute monologue—seemingly fearful that if they stop talking for one second the other person will hang up. News flash: This is not a filibuster, folks. They can end it at *any* time without your permission.

Television provides a good example of creating suspense. During the first few seconds of a show, we have a chance to decide if we're going to continue to watch, change the channel, or pick up a book instead. Television shows and movies must have an element of suspense or mystery in them; otherwise, why would we watch? Sure, there is comfort in seeing the same movie over and over (*Casablanca, The Wizard of Oz, Sleepless in Seattle*) and knowing exactly what's going to happen. But with your client, is there comfort in knowing he is going to have to listen to the same dull sales pitch he's already heard 10 times this week? Would he be more likely to change the channel? Suspense means being uncertain or awaiting an outcome.[1] If your client knows the end of the story, why does he need to see the movie again?

The unsuspenseful sales call

Let's suppose I am calling Bob, a small-business owner who meets my company's profile as a qualified candidate for our new accounting software. Here's how most salespeople would probably approach it:

"Hi Bob. This is Julie Hansen from PDQ Company, and we make accounting software that will cut your bookkeeping time in half. We make the transition from your current system completely effortless, we automatically back up your system on our servers so you never lose data, and we guarantee it for 90 days or your money back. I'd love to come in and show you how our new product will work for you."

Bob hesitates for a moment, thinking this sounds similar to at least five other phone calls he's gotten in the last month, all of which he turned down, and based on what I've said so far, he sees no reason to reevaluate his decision. Besides, haven't I already told him how our product will work for him?

"No thanks. I'm perfectly happy with my current software. Goodbye."

I have been boring and ineffective. So how do I create suspense during that first contact while providing enough information to get in the door?

The suspenseful call

This time, suppose I call Bob up and say "Hi Bob. This is Julie Hansen with PDQ Company and I'm looking for companies who are paying twice as much as they need to in bookkeeping costs. Do you think you might be one of them?"

Bob will probably be taken aback, before quickly recovering and saying something such as "I doubt it! Why would you think my company is paying too much?"

"You'd be surprised. Most companies of your size and billings are putting more of their profits back into accounting systems than they have to because of one little thing. I just helped Peak Enterprises find a way to start turning extraneous accounting costs into profits in less than a month."

Bob is probably at least a *little* intrigued. "How so?"

"I'd love to be able to give you a quick answer over the phone, but as you can imagine, that's really difficult with all the variables involved. It's much faster in person, 15 minutes at the most—and I'm estimating it could possibly save you as much as $5,000 this year alone. I'll be in your area on Friday. Do you have a free 15 minutes around 10 or 10:30?"

First, I've hooked Bob with a disturbing and intriguing idea (I *could be paying twice as much on bookkeeping?! How could she know that?*), I've left out enough information to make him curious (*What is the one thing I could be doing to cut into my profits? Could she really save me $5,000?*), and I've given a plausible reason for being unable to expand any further on the phone (too many variables). What do you think? Did I get the appointment?

Everyone loves a mystery.

How many mysteries or detective shows do you think there are on television right now? A dozen? Fifty? Two hundred? There's a reason we can't get enough of *Law & Order*, *CSI*, and every possible variation of the lawyer and detective story they can think of. People love a mystery, even if someone else solves it for them. If you can create an air of mystery or suspense, you can tap into that part of our human nature that wants to see how the puzzle comes together.

Don't play the end of the scene.

I once played a character who died at the end of the play. During rehearsal, I was dragging my way through an early scene when the director yelled at me: "For God's sake, cheer up! You don't even know you're sick yet!" When an actor starts to telegraph to the audience what happens to his character at the end of the play—good or bad—the audience begins to put it together and guesses the outcome. This is called playing the end of the scene. How many previews have you seen in which, in 30 seconds, you can tell what the entire movie is about, who is going to live or die, and who is going to go on to star in the sequel? Don't play the end of the scene with your prospect. Your job is to provide enough clues to have the CSI team—I mean, your prospect—pick up the trail (more on drama and creating suspense in Chapter 7).

A SALES PRO SCENE: GETTING THE APPOINTMENT

THE CAST

MICHELE: An account manager for a manufacturing prod-
    ucts distributor.

BART: A former account manager for the same distributor

RON: A product manager for one of the top-50 food pro-
    cessing companies in the United States.

THE SETTING

Michele has been assigned to call on a large food processing company after Bart, the previous account manager, quit.
Bart had gotten nowhere with the purchasing agent who does
the actual buying, so for six months, he had been directing
his efforts toward Ron, the ultimate decision-maker, with
no success. Michele's manager believes that Michele can
break this streak, but Michele's not so sure. Bart seemed
to follow every recommended sales tactic: reaching out
via e-mail and phone, sending industry-related articles,
client success stories, and updates on new technology.
Michele knows that she needs to do something different to
    get in to see Ron, but she's just not sure what.

DIRECTOR'S SCENE NOTES:

JH
What is your strategy for the call?

MICHELE
I am going to tell him that we have a new product that has
saved some of his competitors money, and ask for a meeting
    to talk about his needs and how we can meet them.

                              JH

That sounds similar to Bart's approach. What are you going
to do differently that is going to make Ron want to meet
                        with you?

                           MICHELE

Well...I think I'm calling at a good time. I found out
that one of his pieces of equipment had some problems and
this new product we carry can resolve the issue better than
                 anything else that's out there.

                              JH
              So his needs are pretty clear.

                           MICHELE
            Yes, and I was going to get into that.

                              JH

It seems to me that should be your lead story—as opposed
to trying to set up a fact-finding meeting. Can you imagine how many sales reps want to sit down and talk to him
                      about his needs?

                           MICHELE
                           A lot.

                              JH

So let's talk about how you're going to create enough interest to get you in the door. Based on what you know
        about his situation, what are the potential costs?

                           MICHELE

Well, there's the cost of repairs every time his equipment goes down and the cost of lost production. It can
                   get very expensive.

                              JH

And how does your company or this new product solve that?

                           MICHELE

First of all, we have a team of some of the best engineers
in the industry available to work with him to ensure that
this is the best solution for his needs, and secondly, this
new product achieves much higher production level standards and has saved one of his competitors nearly 5 percent
               on their production costs already.

JH

Based on that, lets role-play the call. I'll be Ron.

MICHELE

Hi Ron, this is Michele with XM Distributing and I wanted to let you know about a new product we have that is the best in the industry for preventing the kind of failure you recently experienced.

JH

Thanks but we've got it handled.

MICHELE

But this new product has been able to save one of your competitors as much as 5 percent in production costs.

JH

You can send any information you have to our purchasing agent.

MICHELE

We have, but he's never given us the opportunity to show him how we can address your needs.

JH

Well, send it along and I'll try and mention it to him. I have a meeting now. Goodbye. So Michele, what do you think happened here?

MICHELE

I tried to get in all the information that would be relevant to him. I'm not sure what else I could do.

JH

The information is good, but what you want to do is get in the door, right?

MICHELE

Right.

JH

I think there is a more suspenseful and engaging way to do that. Let's try role-playing again, this time with you playing Ron.

MICHELE

This is Ron.

JH

Hi Ron, Julie with XM Distributing. I was sorry to hear about your recent equipment failure. I know how expensive that can be to have to stop production for that long.

MICHELE

Well...yes. How do you know that?

JH

I make it my job to keep up on what's happening in your industry. Especially since we started carrying a new line of products that addresses that very problem. Tyson has been using this latest technology and has found it saves them as much as 5 percent in production costs.

MICHELE

Sounds interesting. Why don't you send that to my purchasing agent?

JH

To be honest Ron, I've found that purchasing agents can't fully appreciate the value of having just the right product in place to prevent these kinds of problems in the future. I bet no one cares more about that than you do, right?

MICHELE

That's for sure. But listen, we already have the problem fixed.

JH

I know your time is valuable and I wouldn't be calling you if I didn't fully believe that we have a better solution to your problem. I have some of the best engineers in the industry available to come out with me next week, take a look at your equipment, and ensure that we can help you like we helped Tyson. Is there a time that works for you next Thursday or Friday?

MICHELE

I guess I have some time on Friday.

```
                         JH
    Great! So how did you feel about that, Michele?

                      MICHELE
You  kind  of  took  me  by  surprise  in  the  beginning!
                         JH
That's the idea.  If you open with the same script everyone
else uses, he's going to fall into his same script, which
is going to be some version of "send it to my purchasing
                       agent."

                      MICHELE
                      Right.
```

EXERCISES

1. Create a powerful "Moment Before" using the steps outlined in this chapter for your next prospecting call.

2. Write down your expectations for the call. Be brutally honest with yourself.

3. Determine the best-case scenario and adjust your expectations accordingly.

4. Evaluate your current opening for mystery and suspense.

5. Rework your opening, purposely leaving out a key element that can only be revealed when you see the prospect in person. Remember: It must be of value to your prospect, and there must be a plausible reason why you can not divulge it on the phone at that moment.

THE WARM-UP: ACTING EXERCISES FOR SELLERS

4

"The best actors do not let the wheels show."

~Henry Fonda

Heather traveled five days a week, covering a three-state territory for an upstart telecommunications company. She was always rushing from plane to taxi, from appointment to hotel. She would run through her client notes in the elevator, send e-mails and texts while waiting in the lobby, and return calls in the back of a cab. Often, she would find herself at her last appointment of the day, breathless, hoarse, and exhausted. She had finally run out of steam. After a disappointing quarterly review, Heather knew something had to change, but what? She couldn't possibly work any harder.

I helped Heather see that setting aside 7 minutes to prepare in the morning would more than pay off in the time she felt she was losing. We established a physical, vocal, and mental warm-up that would be quick and easy for her to commit to no matter where she was. Soon, it became second-nature for her to do her warm-up before she left her house or hotel, review her goals, and run through her script in the taxi or on the train and focus her mind on the presentation as she waited for her client in the lobby.

Heather and her sales manager were amazed; without changing anything else, she's improved her closing percentage by nearly 50 percent, and has more energy at the end of each day to enjoy other aspects of her life.

In this chapter, you will learn the same techniques that actors use to prepare for competitive auditions and practical tips on how to apply them in your busy day.

Acting techniques to prepare for sales calls:

✪ The physical warm-up.

✪ The vocal warm-up.

✪ The mental warm-up.

✪ The waiting room warm-up.

✪ The seven-minute power warm-up.

YOUR GREATEST SELLING TOOL

What is your greatest selling tool? Is it your Website, your brochure, your multi-media presentation in 3D? Though all of these great technical advances can support you and your message, the answer lies much closer to home: *You* are your greatest selling tool: your mind, your voice, your physicality. Most sales are still won and lost by human beings. Actors refer to this as their instrument. Just as a professional pianist must ensure that his piano is performance-ready, professional salespeople must ensure that their instruments are in top condition.

"How do you get to Carnegie Hall?" Practice. Practice. Practice. Actors rehearse not just for a role, but to prepare for the *possibility* of *maybe, some-day* getting a role. Great actors make it look effortless, but days, months, and often years of training are the gritty truth behind their magic. How do most salespeople prepare for a sales presentation or call? We *cram* ourselves full of information and knowledge on the company, the product, the competition. We *develop* a PowerPoint presentation that would impress NASA. We *run through* our script five minutes before the meeting. But do we spend any time at all preparing ourselves, our instrument for delivering our message? I'll wager that on many occasions, many of us have woken up in the morning, gotten ready for work, slammed down a cup of coffee, and before we've even talked to a soul (including the dog), we've picked up the phone and made a sales call or shown up at an appointment to meet a client or new prospect.

In order to be at peak performance, professional athletes don't show up for the game without stretching and professional singers don't go on stage without vocalizing, so why should we, professional salespeople, go on the business stage without warming up? If you want to give a memorable and effective performance, you must, as actors do, develop a consistent training program for your most important sales tool: yourself.

An Actor's Preparation

Much of an actor's preparation is done well ahead of the audition, in classes and workshops, at home with scene partners, or on their own, and it doesn't stop at the casting director's door. Walking into the waiting area for most casting calls is akin to entering a preschool taken over by the students. Actors are roaming the halls, running scales or lines, mugging (exaggerating facial expressions), stretching, or coaching themselves up. What do you see when you walk into a sales waiting area? Neatly attired men and women sitting very still, legs crossed, smiles firmly planted, eyes glued to their BlackBerrys or perhaps on a glossy magazine temptingly placed in front of them. Which group do you think is more focused and prepared to spring into action? Though their methods are varied, professional actors have a single-minded sense of purpose in their warm-up: They prepare their bodies and minds to be fully ready to communicate the objectives of the role for which they are competing.

In order to win the part, actors must be physically, verbally, and mentally prepared. In sales, we are also competing for a part, yet we are rarely schooled in how to prepare ourselves in these areas to ensure our message is communicated as effectively as possible.

Your Client Is Your Audience

No good actor would dream of going out on stage and warming up in front of his audience. Once the curtain rises or camera rolls, an actor must be on, or he will lose his audience. In sales, you have an audience as well. Your clients or your prospects are your audience. Do you want to risk losing them by spending the first crucial minutes of contact working the kinks out of your performance and getting your brain and mouth in gear? If it's true what experts say, that people form a first impression of us in as little as seven seconds, how many times have you failed the Seven-Second Client Test? Like any kind of professional performer, we need to be warmed up and ready to go *before* we pick up the phone or walk into a potential client, or customer's office. Spending as little as seven minutes a day warming up can make a huge difference in your ability to communicate at your highest potential on every call.

An Actor's Warm-Up

An actor's warm-up is typically broken up into three areas: physical, vocal, and mental. What follows is a compilation of my favorite and most effective exercises for each area that can be done at home or even in waiting rooms, as well as a complete seven-minute power warm-up that you can easily work into your daily routine.

Physical warm-up

You may not think of selling as requiring much physical effort (except the occasional race to an appointment), but being physically loose and free allows you the breath and energy necessary to communicate your ideas and proposals effectively and persuasively. Breathing, releasing tension, and creating energy are the major components of the physical warm-up.

Breathing

Communication rides on the breath; it is the base of every great performance. If you're not breathing properly, you are wasting energy and not thinking at your best. If you're feeling stress these days (and who isn't?) it's probably affecting the way you breathe. Do you ever feel like you're breathing and speaking from the neck up—or even find yourself holding your breath? Proper breathing is from the diaphragm, or belly breathing, as they call it in yoga. Place a hand under your rib cage and breathe in until you feel it moving. Correct breathing gets the oxygen flowing, stimulates alpha brainwaves, helps us think more clearly, and quickens our ability to respond. We can accelerate this oxygenation process by breathing rhythmically, otherwise known as energy breathing:

1. Breathe in through the nose for four counts.

2. Hold for four counts.

3. Breathe out through the mouth for eight counts.

4. Repeat.

Tension

Famous Russian director and father of modern acting Constantin Stanislavski believed that tension was the greatest enemy of the actor. Performing, he said, demanded a state of physical relaxation in which the actor uses only enough muscular tension to accomplish what is necessary.[1] As performers on the business stage, we also need to be relaxed and free of tension in order to achieve our goal. Tension interferes with the free flow of communication by using muscles or energy on areas not involved in the process of delivering our message, thus diluting the power of our words.

For instance, if you typically hold tension in your neck, a fair amount of your attention and energy is being used trying either to relieve that tension or attempting to ignore it. Sometimes we are so used to carrying pain or tension that we are not even consciously aware of it. Either way, the physical or mental energy we are expending takes away our focus and diverts energy from our primary goal: communicating persuasively and precisely.

Lee Strasberg, artistic director for the famous Actor's Studio, believed that relaxation was the foundation on which almost all actors' work was based.[2] He developed a relaxation exercise to help actors identify hidden muscle tension in the body and face and then release it by consciously willing the muscle to "let go."[3] Although this simple procedure may strike you as wishful thinking, give it a chance. You may be surprised at how easily the body responds to a direct command from the mind. Obviously for chronic pain that does not respond, professional attention is recommended.

The relaxation exercise

1. Sit in a straight-backed, armless chair and try to identify tension by focusing on one specific body part at a time, starting with your shoulders.

2. Lift your shoulders up to your ears, rotate them forward and back, asking yourself all the time if you notice any tension.

3. Identify the tense spot or spots, tighten your shoulders up as much as possible, and hold for 10 seconds.

4. Will the muscle to "let go" after 10 seconds, and release. You may need to repeat this several times, especially in very tight areas.

5. Work your way through each area of your body: the neck, arms, hands, chest, stomach, hips, legs, ankles, and feet.

Become a rag doll

Stand up straight, inhale deeply, and, on exhale, start with the top of you head and slowly roll down, one vertebra at a time, until your head and arms are hanging just over your feet. Now shake your arms from side to side, keeping your neck loose at all times. Then inhale, and slowly roll up one vertebra at a time until you are standing with good posture.

Exercises for face and mouth

Extra focus needs to be given to the facial muscles, because hidden tension is often broadcast on the face for everyone to see, even though we may be completely unaware of it. A lot of these exercises should be done in the privacy of your own home—unless you want an empty seat next to you on the bus or train!

1. Little face/big face: Scrunch your face up as tightly as you can, like those little people you used to make out of dried apples in the third grade. Hold it for a moment, then release, making your face as wide as possible, opening your mouth, your eyes, your ears, and so on. Repeat.

2. Forehead lifts: Move the eyebrows up and down rapidly, hold. Repeat a few times until they move easily.

3. Jaw stretch: Open your mouth as wide as you can, extend the jaw, and rotate it around. Change directions after a few rotations. On the final rotation, stop at any area where you feel real tension, tighten, will it to release, and let go.

4. Mouthing off: Move your lips from side-to-side, then in and out. Follow this by sticking your tongue out and moving it around in circles, then in and out.

5. Horsing around: It's one of the first sounds we learned to make as babies and it's one of my "go to" warm-up moves that I use throughout the day to release tension in my face. To quote Lauren Bacall in *To Have and to Have Not*, "Simply put your lips together and blow." Keep the lips and jaw loose, and feel the vibration. This relaxes the muscles around your mouth and is an excellent and easy way to loosen things up, especially if you've been talking a lot.

Vocal warm-up

Each of us has a unique voice, but we may not be using it to its full advantage. Properly warming it up will help you communicate with ease and have people listening to you with rapt attention, as opposed to straining to hear you, or worse, tuning you out.

Sellers often think that if they've been talking all day, their voice is warmed up. That is not necessarily the case. You may not be using your mouth, your vocal chords, and your breath to showcase your voice at its best. In fact, you may be hurting your voice by straining, you may be stuck in a monotone delivery, or you may be speaking too quietly or breathlessly to be effective. By spending a little time warming up each part of the mouth, your true voice will begin to emerge, and you will expand your vocal range, which will add variety to your speech and help avoid the "tune-out" factor. Proper speech is not only easily heard and understood, but can add an extra punch of power to your presentation.

Mouth warm-ups

Repeat each of these sound exercises several times:

Lips: "ba-ba-ba pa-pa-pa"

Tongue: "ta-ta-ta da-da-da"

Back of throat: "ka-ka-ka ga-ga-ga"

☆ Tongue twisters. Try saying each one of these several times in a row, getting faster and faster. You'll find that you are working different parts of your mouth and tongue with each. Over-enunciate to really get precise with each word:

★ Sushi chef.

★ Toy boat.

★ Worldwide web.

★ Round the rough and rugged rock the ragged rascal ran.

★ Unique New York.

★ And my favorite: While one blue bear bled black, the other black bear bled blue.

☆ Octave slides: Take a deep breath and start on a vowel sound, such as "ahh." Start at your lowest register and slowly slide up the scale to the top of your register. (Unless you are an opera singer, this will not be pretty.) Inhale, then repeat, this time sliding down the scale. Next, try it with different vowel sounds, such as "eee" or "ohh." You can get fancy and try sliding up and down all on the same breath, like a roller coaster.

Octave roll down combination

Combine the octave slides with the rag doll roll down as follows: Start on your high note "ahhh," slowly rolling your body down one vertebra at a time until your head and arms are hanging over your feet. You should finish just as you hit your low note. Take a breath, reverse, and come back up, hitting your high note as you come to fully upright.

Connect your voice to your body

News anchors are often called "talking heads," people who are relaying information without any feeling or conviction. It can also refer to people whose bodies seem to be running on separate instructions, independent of their voice and emotions. In order to be persuasive and make an impact, it's important to communicate with your whole being. Each part should be involved in delivering the message and working together as a whole. This does not mean being in a constant state of motion while you're talking, like a fidgety child, but rather having the entire body support your message and ready to perform and add to it, if required.

An added benefit of incorporating the body in your communication is that gesturing has been linked to better speaking. In a recent study at Canada's University of Alberta Augustana College, scientists found that the very act of moving our hands around helps us recall what we're saying and access our language easier.[4] And I don't know about you, but I ah...um, what's the word I'm looking for? Oh yes. I *need* all the help I can get!

Punch it out

Make a fist and punch the air while shouting a hard consonant sound like "pa" or "ba." Imagine throwing your voice to the other side of the room with each jab.

Sales pitch hop

Say your sales pitch as you jump around the room, throw punches, or pretend to skip rope. Don't worry about getting it exactly right or talking in complete sentences; just talk, move, and remember to breathe. (This is not only a great warm-up, but an excellent way to energize scripts, which will be discussed in Chapter 6.)

Mental and emotional warm-up

Now you're loose, energized, and vocally ready to go. Head straight for the phone, right? Whoa there, Trigger! Without the proper mental and emotional focus, we can still miss our target completely. A focused and positive mind creates focused and positive results. Learning how to let go of negativity and get in an ideal state of mind greatly increases your potential for success, and it feels a heck of a lot better! Take a few minutes now to make sure you have the necessary focus and clarity with these exercises.

Emotional dump

This is where you get to express all of your frustrations, disappointments, and unmet needs and wishes (in other words, your daily baggage) until depleted. It is the cheapest form of therapy you will ever have. But instead of using words, which we are sometimes hesitant to say out loud (even when we are alone), we use gibberish. Gibberish is a tool used in many acting and improv classes precisely because it frees us up to express ourselves without getting hung up on the words. It takes the focus off of the actual words and puts it where it should be: on the meaning and intent of what you're saying.

1. Stand up and, stream-of-consciousness-style, spit out your grievances and gripes using any made up words that you like. Your gibberish may sound like a German general, a beautiful European language, or a badly dubbed kung fu movie. Mine sounds suspiciously like pig Latin. It's important not to over-think it or judge; no one is watching and there is no wrong or right way to do it. This should be fun and freeing.

2. Add gestures while you're talking in gibberish—anything that helps you express your frustrations: pump your fists at the sky, kick, scream, jump up and down. Continue to do this until you feel like you've said all you need to say.

There. Feel better? That will be $150, please.

Pre-call energy booster

Making a sale sometimes feels like a sprint, sometimes a marathon. Either way, it requires energy. Although we've been working on relaxing, don't confuse that with being sleepy or groggy. We are striving to keep our energy high and our bodies and minds focused, free of wasteful tension and ready to react—not ready to take a nap on our client's couch. It's true: Move the body, and the mind will follow. Here is a quick way to get our energy flowing:

Shake a leg

Stand up and stretch, reaching up for the sky. Shake an arm. Shake a leg. Hop around. Dance. Do the hokey pokey. Whatever you do, be sure to move loosely and fluidly and engage your whole body. Kill two birds with one stone and do vocal exercises while you move.

Now you can pick up that phone with the confidence that you are ready to perform at your best.

Bonus warm-ups for the waiting room

Waiting rooms are black holes for energy; they can undo most or all of the preparation you've done if you're not careful. Besides draining your energy and dispersing your focus, sitting still for 15 or 20 minutes can give you a bad case of nerves, like an actor waiting anxiously backstage for his cue. So how do you combat this?

1. Put down your BlackBerry or iPhone. Do not check your e-mail, plan for the next appointment, or calculate the commission from this sale. (I know; I've done it, too.) And don't pick up that magazine! Do not get distracted by the many tempting items left out to foil you. Let your competitors fall prey to these traps.

2. Find a quiet place to sit where you can have a little privacy. Be polite to the receptionist and acknowledge others in the room if you must, but remember: The waiting room is *your*

backstage. If you want to alienate a professional actor and blow his performance, try striking up a conversation with him while he's in the wings waiting to go on stage. You need to have that kind of commitment to keeping your focus.

3. Concentrate on three things: your "Moment Before" (from Chapter 3), what you are fighting for (from Chapter 5), and what you are going to do to get it (from Chapter 9).

4. Run through a discreet set of breathing and tension reliever exercises outlined previously in this chapter. Simply breathing into the tight spots and exhaling the tension out is less obvious than moving large muscle groups around.

5. Try humming quietly to yourself. This keeps the vocal chords warmed up and makes the transition from sitting in silence to presenting much smoother.

The 7-minute power warm-up

Everybody can find an extra seven minutes in their morning, right? I've condensed these exercises into a powerful seven-minute warm-up that will not only be effective in making you performance-ready, but also be easy to stick to.

1. Energy Breathing (30 seconds).

2. Relaxation exercise in chair (1 minute).

3. Rag doll (30 seconds).

4. Shake a leg (30 seconds).

5. Facial exercises (1 minute).

   ★ Little face/big face.

   ★ Forehead lifts.

   ★ Jaw stretch.

   ★ Mouth-off.

   ★ Horse around.

6. Vocalize (1 minute). Repeat the following:

   ★ Ba-ba-ba-pa-pa-pa.

   ★ Ta-ta-ta-da-da-da.

   ★ Ka-ka-ka-ga-ga-ga.

- ★ Sushi chef (5x).
- ★ Toy boat (5x).
- ★ Worldwide web (5x).

7. Octave roll down combination (30 seconds).
8. Sales pitch hop (1 minute).
9. Gibberish emotional dump (1 minute).

ACT II:
The Curtain Up

THE MOTIVATION: DISCOVERING POWER GOALS

5

"Acting is doing, because everything you say or do is some kind of an action, some kind of a verb. You're always connected to the other person through some kind of action."

~Mira Sorvino

Jake was pulling down six figures selling printing equipment when the industry hit the brakes. Easy money turned into hard work, and Jake grew increasingly impatient and unhappy. After going through the discovery process in this chapter, Jake was able to uncover a strong personal motivation that would propel him to seek new ways to overcome market and industry conditions rather than run from them. As his focus became clear, his state of mind and outlook improved, and gradually so did his billing. Soon Jake was more than making up for his losses with new business opportunities.

There's nothing inherently wrong with financial motivation, but without an equally powerful emotional purpose, how much effort will you consistently put in to your career—especially if the money starts to slow down or the competition heats up? Will you be one of the multitudes of salespeople who jump from job to job in search of that winning trifecta of right product, right client, and right timing? Sure, you may get lucky and ride the wave for years. But watch out when the tsunami comes—as it surely has in this new economy. Will you run for cover, or take your cues from dedicated actors, and continue to hone your skills and find new ways to adjust and grow?

Acting techniques for finding and using motivation:

☆ Knowing what you are fighting for.

☆ Scoring your role.

☆ Selecting action words.

☆ Communicating in the moment.

☆ Visualizing and sense memory.

The average income of the 100,000 actors in the Screen Actors Guild is less than $5,000 a year.[1] The number of actors auditioning for roles well exceeds the number of available parts, forcing the majority of actors to support themselves through other means while continuing to work on their craft. For most dedicated actors, money is rarely the chief motivator. If it were, you can bet there would be a lot fewer actors in the world! Why do they do it? What drives them to devote so much time and energy to the pursuit of something with so little chance for financial reward?

As salespeople, we would quickly turn and run from such odds. In fact, I would wager that financial reward is one of the major reasons people choose a career in sales. It's nothing to be ashamed of. It's part of the American dream. Certainly there are other factors that lead one in to sales: excitement, variety, freedom, working with people, creative problem-solving. But let's be honest: Couldn't you achieve some of those same things working for Greenpeace or the United Nations? So let's talk about money.

FINANCIAL MOTIVATION EQUALS EFFICIENCY

Say it along with me: "Sales is a numbers game." It's drilled into us from day one on the job. It takes a certain amount of *no's* before you get to a *yes*. When approaching anything from a strictly financial motive, efficiency becomes your master. Any performance driven by efficiency, whether acting or selling, creates cookie-cutter behavior, rote speech, and limited time devoted to creative problem-solving.

Popular research shows that 60 percent of all sales are made after the fourth call. However, 44 percent of reps quit after the first call and another 24 percent after the second call. Only 12 percent of salespeople make more than four calls.[2] In fact, one study shows that the average number of phone attempts a salesperson makes on a company-provided lead is 1.14.[3] Other statistics on prospecting show that it takes between six and eight calls to reach a decision-maker.[4]

Everyone has a limit to the amount of time and effort they are willing to invest in a sale. With a little self-observation, you'll recognize when you've reached yours. Unfortunately, so will your customer. It may be after the second or third objection or the fourth unreturned phone call, but at some point, most of us will mentally and emotionally check out. In the middle of a presentation that isn't going well you find yourself devising a quick exit strategy. You're on the phone with a client who is giving you another stall and you catch yourself checking e-mail. How often do you fully commit to seeing the sales call through? How often do you go to the trouble of making that second, third—let alone *eighth* call?! If the answer is less than you care to admit, you're not alone.

Successful sellers who have survived the tides of economic change, committed to their craft all the while managing to make a good living and maintaining their sanity, have found something else that drives them. It's something beyond a paycheck. I challenge you to find something deeper as well. What follows are a key set of acting tools to help you lock in strong, personal motives that will keep you focused and committed even in tough times.

WANTING IS A PASSIVE VERB

What do I need to sell to meet my quota? How many calls do I have to make to close a sale? What do I want to make this year? When it comes to goal-setting, the focus is on wants—both the company's and our own. But wanting is passive. It's just a feeling, a need, a desire; it can be strong or weak, but it still has only the *potential* to lead to action. In contrast, acting and selling are active. They put you in a state of *doing*, rather than *being*.

We all have wants. Some are long-term, such as a fancy sports car, a house on the golf course, or a college education for your children. Some are more immediate, such as a hot dog or a cold beer at the baseball game. Many wants are simply wishful thinking. Yes, we want it, but we're not necessarily fully committed to doing what it takes to get it. In fact, if something better, easier to achieve, or more immediate comes along, we readily get knocked off course.

What are you fighting for?

Anna really wanted to sell more, but her actions proved otherwise. Most of her free time was spent on other interests, such as daily workouts, her book club, and her infatuation with the latest reality TV show. When she committed to fighting to sell more, her entire attitude changed. Suddenly, there was almost nothing that would stand in the way of getting a sale. She found her energy more focused and her days more productive, which still left her time for her hobbies and friends.

As famous casting director and author Michael Shurtleff suggests in his book *Audition*, actors must make strong, active choices for motivation in order to keep a scene moving forward. Reframing goals from "What do I want?" to the more powerful "What am I fighting for?" inspires action and increases the stakes.[5]

Wanting that big house on the golf course is one thing, but fighting to get it by doggedly pursuing those 10 extra sales, scrimping and saving, and putting in hours of overtime to actually place a down payment on it is an entirely different mindset. Think back to the last time you fought for something. Was it a job? Was it a relationship? A parking spot? It doesn't matter how trivial it may seem to others; if you are emotionally committed to it or the consequences are of great enough significance, even that first cup of coffee in the morning can be worth fighting for.

When you're fighting, all of your senses are engaged. You are determined and emotionally charged. You are not on the fence. You consider all the possible ways to reach your goal. You charge ahead. You convince. You charm. You commit yourself to attaining A, and you will not settle for B. When you hit a speed bump, you don't head for the first exit. You try different ways of attacking that speed bump: slowing down, going around it, jack-hammering it if you must, but not giving up.

Perhaps you believe that your product or service speaks for itself. Merely presenting its benefits should be sufficient to convince anyone of its superiority. Your emotional commitment is not really necessary. That may be in some cases, but as Shurtleff puts it: "The truth is not enough... unless it is invested with sufficient emotion to make it important."[6] Does your product or service *really* sell itself? If so, I suggest you put this book down immediately and start searching for a new job, as it is only a matter of time before you are replaced with a computerized buying system!

"But I'm only selling paper or tools or widgets," you say. "It's so unimportant, even I find it boring." True, your product may not be the cure for cancer, but if you search hard enough, you will find something that personally connects you to your product or service. Try to answer the following questions and see if you can find something that works for you. Does your product or service:

☆ **Benefit the buyer?** Then get connected. Who is your buyer? What is her personal story? Get to know her. Is your product/service saving her money she can use toward another important need? Is it saving her time that she can spend with her family? How does that make you feel to know you have contributed value to another's life and that of her family?

☆ **Benefit the user?** Who ultimately benefits from your product/service? Put a face on the end user. What's her story? How does she benefit? What would she lose if she did not have access to your product/service?

☆ **Benefit the community?** What does your product/service add to the community locally, nationally, or globally? Think big picture. Are you feeding the economic system by creating jobs? What does it feel like to be a responsible contributor to society? What is that worth to you?

If you still can't find a sufficiently strong motivation to get behind your product or service, you can go back to finding the importance in your own circumstances, as discussed earlier. Think about your personal stakes. Are you fighting to keep your job? Are you fighting for respect? Power? Attention? Do not pretend that you don't care or that you're okay with whatever happens. Personally invest in the outcome. Before Nike adopted "Just do it," Yoda from *Star Wars* offered these great words of wisdom: "Do or do not. There is no try."

<u>WHAT ARE YOU FIGHTING FOR? A SALES PRO SCENE</u>

THE CAST

LOGAN: A senior underwriting associate for a public radio station.

KRISTA: A new underwriting associate at the same station.

THE SETTING

Logan has been selling underwriting sponsorships to local and regional businesses for a public radio station for nine years. Though it is not technically called "advertising," he competes for advertising dollars with dozens of other broadcast stations in the market, most of which offer commercial lengths six times longer than Logan's station's 10-second sponsorship messages. And his competitors' commercial lengths are priced much lower. Logan hears the same objection again and again: "If I can buy another station and reach the same number of people for less money and have more time to get my message across, why should I pay more for your station?" Logan is discouraged and stuck.

DIRECTOR'S SCENE NOTES:

LOGAN

We're not a typical radio station; our audience is extremely loyal and engaged, and continues to grow while many other stations' audiences are shrinking. Despite the quality of the programming and listenership, it often comes down to rates when I get into negotiations and I can't typically compete on that basis. As businesses are struggling to make their bottom line, I'm having a harder time getting clients to value the quality of the listenership over the cost-effectiveness of other media choices.

JH

So tell me what your station is fighting for.

LOGAN

To be our listeners primary news source and to deliver quality programming that keeps them informed and entertained.

JH

And how are you accomplishing that?

LOGAN

We're opening news bureaus across the country and developing innovative new programming while other stations are cutting costs.

JH

What would happen if you cut back on your programming?

LOGAN

Listeners wouldn't get the in-depth type of news stories we are able to offer or have easy access to the programs that they love. They'd have to get their news from other sources: waiting for a live newsbreak on a commercial station, or spending extra time at the end of their day catching up by reading the paper or going online.

JH

That's time they could be spending with their family, right? Going for a bike ride? Watching a movie?

LOGAN

Exactly.

JH

So you provide a public service, a free and convenient community service that helps people stay on top of the most important things going on in their world—as they are happening. Why is it important that you provide the type of in-depth news coverage and quality of programming that you do?

LOGAN

There are a lot of important stories out there that aren't being told or given proper attention. Our listeners appreciate that we dig deeper than the headlines and bring them stories that they won't get elsewhere. They like to be challenged and informed.

JH

How do you think your listeners feel about a service that they can rely on to provide all of that simply in exchange for listening to a few sponsorship mentions each hour?

LOGAN

They have a great sense of loyalty and goodwill for us, which is consistently reflected in our ratings and feedback from our listeners.

JH

And because they are getting that information from a source they trust and rely on, your client, the sponsor, is also the recipient of that goodwill.

LOGAN

True. But most businesses today are far more interested in making a quick sale than building goodwill.

JH

What value do you think business owners place on goodwill for their own business?

LOGAN

A great deal—if they're smart! A loyal, lifelong customer is worth 20 times that of a one-time buyer.

JH

I think you've just given a very good answer to why your station is worth more. Don't you? Now what about you? What are you fighting for?

LOGAN

Well, I'd like to close more business.

JH

You'd *like* to?

LOGAN

Let me rephrase that. I am *fighting* to close more business.

JH

Why?

LOGAN

I need to make my quota.

JH

Not strong enough.

LOGAN

I'm down in billing. Krista, who's fairly new to the station, is about to pass me for the year.

JH

So there's competition. How do you feel about some new person who hasn't paid their dues waltzing in and taking your spot at the top?

LOGAN

Well, I don't like it. I want to be the top biller.

JH

You *want* to?! What are you *fighting* for? Be positive and specific.

LOGAN

I'm fighting to be on top. To prove I'm still the best.

JH

There you go.

Scoring Your Role

After determining the overarching goal they are fighting for in a play, actors must continue to search for an objective in each scene and a motive for each series of actions or dialogue. This is typically referred to as "scoring the role," or breaking a script down into "beats," which can be thought of as single units of action. There is something that drives everything we say and do. Therefore to communicate clearly and effectively, our external words and actions must be in sync with our internal goals. We need to be connected to what we are saying or doing. Otherwise we are at risk of blindly parroting someone else's words and feigning feeling or emotion—the antithesis of modern acting or selling.

A director instructs an actor to walk across the stage, pick up a glass, and say his line.

Actor: What's my motivation?

Director: Your paycheck.

The actor in the joke (originally attributed to Alfred Hitchcock) lacked a good, specific reason for his action. Therefore, he must find his own. Most likely he is thirsty. Or perhaps he has a bad taste in his mouth from the cigar he just smoked. Or maybe he is stalling so he can think of a response to a particularly challenging question. There are an infinite number of motives for any single sentence or action. It is up to the actor and the salesperson to find the strongest motive to inspire a committed pursuit of his goal.

Don't Forget Your Scene Partner

An actor's motivation is also influenced by the interaction with his scene partner. Who is your scene partner in sales? Your customer! And because your customer brings his or her own needs and wants into the scene, a beat goal must be flexible and possible variations explored beforehand in improvisational or role-playing exercises.

Perhaps during a particular section or beat of your presentation, your goal is to *convince* the buyer that your product is the best value for the price. The buyer interrupts, telling you about a particularly bad experience he had with the product several years ago. Instead of dismissing his comments and forging ahead with your pitch, you quickly shift to a new goal, to *prove* your product's reliability or to *demonstrate* your company's exemplary record in customer satisfaction.

Let's look at how major goals break down into beats by comparing some examples of central characters from film and theater to two common sales situations: *discovering* client satisfaction level with current vendor to *challenging* client to expect more.

Chart 1: A comparison of acting vs. selling goals

	Main Goal	Scene Goal	Beat Goal
Movie Example: Rocky Balboa in *Rocky:*	to *earn* respect	to *win* Adrian's love	to *convince* her to go out with him
Sales Example 1:	to *reclaim* business lost to competitor	to *reposition* product	to *demonstrate* new features
Theater Example: Sophie in *Mama Mia!:*	to *find* dad to give her away at wedding	to *gather* potential fathers in one place	to *encourage* father to reveal himself
Sales Example 2:	to *increase* sales volume by 10 percent through new business	to *discover* client satisfaction level with current vendor	to *challenge* client to expect more

SELECTING ACTION WORDS

"The talent is in the choices."~Robert DeNiro

Now that you've discovered what you're fighting for and what motivates you—both overall and from moment-to-moment—how are you going to achieve your goal? Even with strong motivation and commitment, if no action is taken, nothing happens in the scene or the sale. The audience is bored and leaves at intermission. The client makes up an excuse, and you leave empty-handed.

As an actor, I learned the importance of the language I used to motivate myself and direct my actions on stage—and it's just as critical in business. Actors are always looking for the strongest choices for their characters. Weak characters with unclear actions and goals aren't interesting to watch, and neither are weak salespeople. The more specific and powerful the words you choose, the more focused and powerful your actions.

According to the *Oxford English Dictionary*, there are 171,476 words in current use, and about 25,000 of these are verbs. Those are a lot of words to choose from; However, most of us end up using the same words over and over—even when they have failed to inspire us in the past. This particular form of insanity (doing the same thing over and over, but expecting different results) is as rampant in business as it is in other areas of our lives. But fortunately, by reading this book, you have made a commitment to becoming a conscious salesperson. You are becoming increasingly aware of your motives and actions and being honest with yourself about the results. It is through this new awareness that you will be able to experiment with new actions by trying them in the different scenes of your life, monitoring their effectiveness.

This simple trick of replacing habitual actions with stronger, clearer action words can trigger a whole new attitude, focus your energy, and stimulate creativity. Think of the power of the words *Seize the day* spoken by Robin Williams's character in *Dead Poets Society*. This 1989 movie inspired a group of students to reach for greatness and more than 20 years later inspired more than four million search results on Google.

Chart 2 contains a partial list of potential selling actions to stimulate your imagination. Try one on for size. For example, see if you notice a difference in your attitude or energy when you focus on *unveiling* a feature as opposed to just *telling* someone about it.

Chart 2: Potential selling actions

advice	agree	appeal	assess	assure	attest
challenge	charm	clarify	coax	conclude	confirm
confront	convince	debunk	defend	demonstrate	deliver
describe	develop	discuss	dispel	display	document
dramatize	elaborate	emphasize	enable	encourage	establish
expand	explain	explore	express	focus	forge
give	help	highlight	identify	illustrate	incorporate
indulge	integrate	introduce	invent	investigate	jolt
justify	link	list	maintain	mention	motivate
move	name	note	observe	offer	outline
persuade	pinpoint	point out	portray	predict	prescribe
present	petition	probe	prod	prompt	propose
prove	question	recommend	reconstruct	recount	reinforce
refer	reject	relate	remind	report	respond
reveal	review	scrutinize	shake up	share	shift
show	specify	speculate	stimulate	stress	substantiate
suggest	summarize	sum up	supply	surprise	tackle
tease	test	unearth	unify	unveil	urge
use	validate	vindicate	warn	woo	work out

3 key factors for selecting a selling action

1. Identify what verbs you are using. Pay attention to that silent dialogue in your head. Do you reflexively pick up the phone to *tell* a client about your product, or do you make a conscious decision to call and *excite* them? Do you *show* your customer how you can save them money, or do you go in armed with the determination to *prove* it? The way you talk to yourself and the words you choose influence your actions and your delivery.

2. Replace tired, passive words with powerful, active verbs. Sometimes the right word can refocus you and completely change your mental and physical energy. Stuck for ideas? Refer to Chart 2, or get out your dictionary or thesaurus.

3. Specify how you would put this new word into action. How would you *dramatize* a product's benefit or *surprise* a customer? Here are two examples from common sales scenes:

Defend vs. explore

Scene: A client tells you that a competitor's product appears to be a better choice. Instead of *defending* your product, try *exploring* the client's assertion and help him arrive at the conclusion that your product is more suitable for his needs.

Give vs. establish

Scene: You are *giving* a 20-minute PowerPoint presentation to a new client. In order to keep her engaged throughout your presentation, try *establishing* agreement on each point before moving on to the next.

Negative vs. positive actions

To ensure your motives are powerful and sustainable, make sure that they are in a positive form. Although negative motivations may fuel you for a little while, they can quickly run out of steam, and people tend to respond poorly to them. You may really desire to get even with a particular customer or steal business from a competitor, but those negative emotions will only drain your energy and hurt your effectiveness in the end. Even Norman Bates in *Psycho* had a positive motive: not just to kill guests at his hotel, but to please his mother. (Okay, that's the last comparison between sales and a horror movie you will hear.)

With a little work, any negative action can be turned into its positive counterpart. Brainstorm ways to reposition your action in a positive light. Here are some examples:

Negative	Positive
Argue	Negotiate
Insist	Compel
Demand	Urge
Track down	Pursue
Push	Encourage

THROW OUT THE STAGE (SALES) DIRECTIONS

Well-trained actors balk at stage directions that describe in detail how they should take a certain action, or bristle at directors who tell them how they should deliver a line. They frequently disregard instructions in the script such as "smile *meaningfully*" or "hand over *gladly*." They know that actions motivated by a strong desire and an emotional commitment develop in an organic way, and they are much more truthful and powerful. Even Shakespeare knew this; he gave actors only the simplest directions—*enter* and *exit*—in his many plays.

In the same way, be careful not to predetermine how you will deliver a line or take an action. This usually involves adding a descriptive adverb to your chosen action. Although your motive may be to persuade or convince, resist the urge to get too specific (for example, telling yourself "I'm going to *urgently* persuade" or "ask *forcefully*") Adverbs limit and restrict us in our search for honest and meaningful behavior. Throw them out.

COMMUNICATE IN THE MOMENT

"I really wanted to make that sale!" Lynn cried as we walked out of a big Manhattan ad agency. But having been on the call with her, I was hard-pressed to see it. It is not enough to *know* what your objective is if it is not communicated in the moment it is needed—not an hour earlier in your sales manager's office, not five minutes before in the elevator, and certainly not sitting in your car afterward, banging your head against the steering wheel!

An actor performs when the curtain goes up and the lights go on. He can't afford to take the entire scene to "warm up" and hit his stride. Neither can you. If our prospect is forming an impression of us within seven seconds or less, you need to ask yourself: Am I on by then? The sales call is your show and your time to shine. Every fiber in your being must be prepared, alive, and awake in that moment.

How do we activate that motivation and put that energy to use in our call or presentation? There are a number of ways, including developing a strong "Moment Before," which was covered in Chapter 3, but as Michael Shurtleff succinctly put it in his book, *Audition!*: "...sometimes you just have to flay yourself into feeling." What follows are two important acting techniques that may "flay" you into feeling in order to capture that desire in a visceral and usable way.

Visualization

Visualization is a powerful and proven tool if used correctly and consistently. Much has been written about it, and there are some very helpful books available that I encourage you to read. I will not spend more time on it other than to offer the following advice: Don't let your success be limited by a limited imagination. We are so often focused on one goal and one path to get there that we don't see greater opportunities that present themselves along the way. As Shakti Gawain said in her best-selling book *Creative Visualization*, be sure to add: "This or *something better* is now manifesting for me in totally satisfying and harmonious ways."

If your goal is to win the sale, imagine how that would feel and what that would look like. Then expand your visualization to include more possibilities; not just a sale, but a series of sales; not just a referral, but an ongoing source of new business; not just a client, but a client for life. If this seems too far-fetched for you, start small: Walking into a new prospect's office? Visualize a warm and open reception. Entering a tense negotiating situation where there are sure to be objections? Imagine achieving a successful conflict resolution and a mutually beneficial solution.

Sense memory

If you've ever seen a stage actor cry on cue, howl with laughter, or shriek with pain, you've probably wondered: "How does he do that every night?" There are many different tricks or tools actors use. The one made famous by method acting is sense memory, a formula for stimulating physical and emotional reactions by recalling a memory from one of our five senses associated with a specific event.[7]

Distant memories such as the scent of your grandmother's house, the feel of your baby's skin, or the warmth of a roaring fire can cause an emotional or physical reaction in the present. The imagined smell of cookies may make you hungry and cause your mouth to water, and the imagined scent of your mother's perfume may make you sad or cause you to smile, depending on what memory you associate with it. Pavlov's dog is an example of sense memory. The dog hears a bell every time he is fed, so, after a while, he begins to salivate when the bell rings—before there is any real evidence of food being delivered.

The rationale behind using sense memory is that it is difficult for even the best actors to will their emotions to the surface. If you've ever seen an actor trying to force himself to cry, laugh, or scream, you know firsthand how awkward and unnatural "going for an emotion" can look.

Studies show that memories are typically locked in the subconscious, and often it is only by recalling the stimuli associated with an experience in our past that we can elicit an actual physical and emotional reaction. When recalling the event, imagining as many details from it as possible and using as many of the senses as you can is helpful. Everyone's triggers are different. Some people respond more to sound, whereas others find a visual reminder or a smell to be more powerful. If you experiment with this technique, you will quickly find what works best for you.

To demonstrate, look at how the following challenges to create a particular emotion are handled in both an acting and a selling situation using sense memory.

Acting example

Challenge: An actor is given a scene in which she is expected to cry on cue.

Solution: Instead of recalling a general feeling of sadness, she picks out a specific event that drove her to tears and a sensory experience tied to that event. She thinks about the day her first child was born and the sweet smell of her baby's head when he was handed to her as she lie sweaty and exhausted in the delivery room. She imagines the weight of the soft, warm bundle in her arms, the tiny pink rosebud of a mouth gently quivering as her baby takes its first few breaths on this earth. Soon, the actor's eyes are welling up.

Sales example

Challenge: You must present a new product feature with great enthusiasm, yet you cannot get in touch with the sense of excitement that you would like to share with your client.

Solution: You search for a time when you felt a high level of positive anticipation or excitement. You recall the day you got your first new car: the feel of that shiny silver key in your hand, the smell of new leather as you snuggled down into your bucket seat, the sound of U2's "Beautiful Day" playing on the radio as you pulled out of your garage on the way to show off your new ride to your friends. Soon, you are sailing into your meeting with positive energy and a sense of anticipation.

EXERCISES

1. Use stream of consciousness to unearth what you're fighting for and repeat as many times as necessary: *I feel... I want...*

I need... I am fighting for... filling in the blank with whatever comes to mind. It is important not to edit or judge yourself as you do this and write down everything that resonates with you. What comes up may surprise you. Some of it will be silly and some unrelated to your career, but keep pushing until you get to the real stuff. Write the top three things you are fighting for in a notebook or on an index card. Keep it in your wallet or purse and read it every morning and night, as well as before going into a sales call.

2. Select five active verbs using the list in Chart 2 or a dictionary that could help you achieve your goals. Be creative and, again, don't edit yourself as you go; just think and write it down. Try one each day and note the difference in your attitude, actions, and results.

3. Sense Memory Exercise 1: When you have your morning coffee or tea, pay attention to all the details associated with the experience. Note the taste, touch, smell, sound, and look. Do this for three days. On the fourth day, try to re-create the sensation of holding and drinking your coffee without actually having it there in front of you. Don't have it brewing in the kitchen either—that's cheating! Feel the weight of the cup in your hands; your fingers curled around the handle. Let the smell of the roasted beans waft up into your nose. Taste the warm coffee hitting your lips and your tongue, and finally rolling down your throat. On the fifth day, make your *real* morning coffee and note what you got right and what you missed.

4. Sense Memory Exercise 2: After you've done the first exercise for a week, select a particular emotion that you would like to feel or project during a specific business encounter and take the following steps:

    ★ Recall a specific event where you experienced the desired emotion.

    ★ Make a list of all sensory experiences associated with that event.

    ★ Explore each of the senses to see which one brings up the strongest memory, or physical or emotional reaction for you.

★ Recall a specific emotion, then immediately start rehearsing your sales pitch. Do not try to hold on to the memory or sensation; let it carry into your presentation, and it should create a momentum of its own.

★ Practice, practice, practice!

THE SCRIPT:
FROM MUNDANE
INTO MEMORABLE

6

"Acting has to do with saying it as if you meant it, so for me the words are always very important. It's very important for me to know my lines, know them so well that I don't have to think about them."

~Christopher Walken

Kara and Matt are investment consultants for a large financial services company. They both use the same sales presentation, yet Kara makes her presentation sound fresh and innovative each time. She makes each individual client feel as if her presentation were created specifically for them. She speaks with passion and intention, creating word pictures so vivid that her clients can almost visualize the results in their own lives. Conversely, Matt sounds as if he's given the same presentation for a dozen years without varying a single word: His voice is monotone, he lacks any emotional connection to the material, and he rushes through it as if he had somewhere more important to be. Matt's client wishes he would go there already.

Let's face it: Most sales presentations are heavy on facts, light on entertainment, and full of sales-speak, and yet, they are the best vehicle we have for getting information across to our clients in a way that they will remember and take action on. How can we use our words to get the full potential out of our valuable face or phone time with clients?

The actor's goal is to communicate the message and vision of the writer in a way that engages and affects the audience. To do so, many talented directors and acting coaches have developed a variety of tools to help actors take the words "off the page" and make them come to life in a meaningful and impactful way. When it's done right, it looks easy. Now you can make it look easy, too, by learning the following tricks of the trade that are guaranteed to bring even the dullest of business scripts to life.

Acting techniques for a powerful sales script include:

☆ Add personality to even the most routine business scripts.

☆ Connect emotionally with your material.

☆ Memorize, rehearse, and deliver a script without sounding canned.

☆ Write your own persuasive sales script.

WHY WE HATE BUSINESS SCRIPTS

Q: How many actors does it take to screw in a light bulb?

A: It depends on what it says in the script.

This joke pokes fun at amateur actors who take every stage direction as written in stone: *smile here*, *say angrily*, *walk downstage*, and so on. They are afraid to move or show an emotion unless it's written in the script. Some sellers are also resistant to deviating from their scripted presentation out of fear of losing their place or handling client questions and other types of spontaneous interactions they may not be prepared for. I was on a call with a new salesperson who was interrupted about halfway through his presentation by a client's question. After answering as best he could, I could see him struggling to find his place. As he started to launch into previously covered material, I was able to subtly guide him back to where he'd left off. When we discussed the call later, we were able to identify the problem. He had improperly memorized his script without understanding what he was saying and why—a mistake you won't make if you follow the four simple steps in this chapter.

I find that most sellers avoid using scripts or following written presentations verbatim because the scripts are poorly written or don't match the seller's style, or the seller is afraid of sounding canned or phony. Both of these are valid fears. It is the rare actor who can bring a script to life without applying technique and rehearsal, so imagine the likelihood of amateurs spontaneously pulling it off! Learning a few key script-reading and memorization techniques is more than worth the small investment in time and effort it takes to do so. Mastering the art of delivering a script convincingly and persuasively will dramatically improve your chances of closing a sale.

WHY USE A BUSINESS SCRIPT?

If we're at risk of sounding canned or phony, why use a script in the first place? Because within your company or industry, your marketing director, sales manager, or a coach has put time and thought into the language, the content, and the order. Through trial and error, experience and/or research, they have come up with their best plan for covering all of the necessary selling points in a way that will maximize its impact and lead to a sale. If they are really good, they have probably also factored in allowances for basic human nature and a variety of typical responses. I'm not saying that you are not uniquely brilliant, creative, and intuitive, but consider that a script just may be *slightly* more well thought-out and reliable than what you can come up with on the fly.

Your company may have one primary sales script for your product or service, or it may have one for every possible selling situation, from prospecting to closing. Real estate coach Mike Ferry offers more than 25 free scripts on his Website for everything from listing a property for sale by owner to prospecting at an open house.[1] Some companies offer only selling points and guidelines; others may provide specific instructions for what to say, when to say it, and how to say it. If the client says yes, proceed to Response 3. If the answer is no, go back to Response 1. It's like playing a business version of Chutes & Ladders! I know of several coaching systems that indicate on each line where to smile, pound your fist, nod, or stand when speaking to a prospect on the phone or in person. Although that type of direction should be reserved for the eighth-grade class play, resist the urge to throw out the baby with the bath water. Scripts can give us a framework on which to build our own distinct presentation.

How to say it

Lest you think I am a script-freak and use one for everything from saying "hello" to "I'll have the Caesar salad," I am well aware that few business scripts are written in a style or language that suits us. In fact, most seem to be written by someone who enjoys kicking back with a well-worn thesaurus. As an actor, I would often get a script and think, "I would never say that!" Yet somehow, I would indeed have to say it—and not only say it—but attempt to make the words sound as if they were my own. (Writers tend to get a little testy when you leave things out or make up your own words: "My kingdom for a….hamburger?") The beauty of sales is that there is no writer watching in the wings to make sure you don't change any of his precious words and no director yelling "Cut!" if you improvise or drop a line. (There are tips for working with the occasional control-happy sales managers who demand word-for-word delivery in Chapter 16.)

In my first stage performance, I was cast as a nurse in an original play and had this single line to deliver: "Doctor, his condition is perplexing." Up until this time, I had never used the word *perplexing* in a sentence, so it seemed like a stone rolling around in my mouth. It was as if I were suddenly speaking like a bad Shakespearean actor. No matter how many times I practiced it—and practice it I did: in the shower, in the car, at the gym—I still felt like a little girl wearing her mother's high heels and pearls every time I said it. On opening night, I spit out the dreaded line and an interminable silence followed, interrupted at last by a few snickers from the audience, and though they will not admit it, I recognized the muffled laughs of at least one or two of my closest friends. This was not the reaction I was hoping for, but I couldn't really blame them. I hadn't found the key to making the language fit me, and for that, everyone had to suffer.

I've run across many lines since then that, on first read, seem just as unlikely to roll off my tongue with any sort of ease, but I've learned some powerful techniques that have helped me to weave even the most awkward sentences into my vocabulary. It's not unlike an actor taking on a role that requires an accent. At first it feels strange and unnatural, but after correct practice, you find yourself slipping into it naturally, freeing you to place the focus where it belongs, on the meaning and intent of what you're saying, rather than the sound of the words.

Admittedly, most sales scripts are neither Shakespeare or Mamet. Sadly, they are more often dated and dull (*What will it take to get you into this car today, Mr. Buyer?*). The good news is that you can still use them as a blueprint for building a presentation that is best suited to your individual selling style. In order to personalize your script, there are four simple steps you must take.

4 simple steps for working with a script

"The whole essence of learning lines is to forget them so you can make them sound like you thought of them that instant." ~Glenda Jackson

Just as an actor receives a play once he gets the part, we are given either a fully written presentation or a set of facts and objectives to communicate to our client. In both cases, we will call this our script. Let's look at what a professional actor does when he first receives a script and see how we can apply those tools as sellers.

Step 1: The initial read-through

The actor reads through the entire play (not just his part), keeping an open mind, and letting ideas and perceptions develop on their own without setting anything in stone. Most sellers (and many actors) stop right here and jump straight to memorization, trying out different ways of saying lines or words. Be forewarned: This will result in a superficial, mechanical performance that will persuade very few and wow no one.

Step 2: The answer to key questions

After reading his scene several times, the actor asks himself key questions, such as: What is this play about? What is at stake? What is the writer trying to convey? What is my point of view? He asks himself how each particular scene ties into the play as a whole, getting more and more specific as he goes. As a seller, this would translate into questions such as: What is this presentation about? What is at stake for my client? What is my company trying to get across? How does this fit into the bigger picture for my client?

Step 3: The identification

The actor must start to identify with the script. If he is not familiar with the facts or is not provided facts by the writer, he must do research or try to relate to a situation through his own personal experience or imagination. Sellers also need to research any facts or sources that their script relies on or makes reference to, and make sure that they fully understand them. Not only will that ensure a believable delivery, but it will also add to their own self-confidence and allow them to explain it to their clients without struggling, if necessary.

Step 4: The breakdown

The actor does a breakdown of the script. This is similar to "Scoring the Role" in the previous chapter where the actor breaks down the script into "beats" or individual meanings for each line or related group of lines. This is often referred to as finding the subtext. The line in our sales script might read: *Our new model comes with a lifetime guarantee.* We ask ourselves what the real meaning and intent of the line are. The answer is to put the customer at ease, to eliminate the fear of making a major purchase. We must be thorough and specific in order to fully bring the script to life. The following three steps make it easy to break down any script:

1. **Focus on intent.** Forget the face value of the words for a moment and focus on the intention of each line. If you are asking someone "What are you doing to market your home?" are you really curious and hoping to pick up some new marketing tips, as that question implies? Or are you trying to drive home the point that without proper marketing, he's not going to get his home sold? Do not be vague or rush past any line because you are already familiar with it. If you don't know why you're saying something, if it doesn't ring true or make sense to you, you need to research it, revise it, or drop it. Otherwise, you may as well be reading from the phone book. Sample line from sales script: *We reach 200,000 active listeners every week.* What you're really saying: *With that many listeners, you can be assured of reaching a large number of potential customers who are in the market for your product at any given time.*

2. **Say it as you would say it.** Get across the "intent" of the words and eliminate unnecessary buzz words or industry jargon. Line from sales script: *We provide you with comparative market data and pricing recommendations.* Rephrased line: *I can show you how you stand in relation to the rest of your competitors and help you come up with a price that will move your house quickly.*

3. **Know what you want.** When you say your line or ask your question, know what type of response you are looking to receive. Do you want agreement? Do you want to encourage questions? Be clear. If you don't know what you want, you won't know when you get it. Sample line from sales script: *Most of our clients sign up for the three-year plan.* What you want: To prove credibility and convince them to purchase the plan.

How to rehearse a sales script

After following the previous four steps, breaking down your script into meaningful "bites" and fully understanding your intent and expectations, the temptation will be to jump in and start memorizing it from the top down. It is critical to resist the urge and follow these steps, which will allow you to develop the material naturally. It will have greater significance to you, you won't struggle over lines, words, and meanings, and you will be freed up in the moment to be at your most persuasive and dynamic. And you will be less likely to forget it or get lost.

Before I made the connection that the rehearsal technique I used in acting could also benefit me in sales, I would spend hours trying to memorize my proposal verbatim, page-by-page, or slide-by-slide. One particular presentation was especially complex. I had just begun working for a marketing company that sold signage and promotional programs at vacation destinations when I got a meeting with the account team for a national sports product line. By the time I arrived at the company's campus in New Jersey, I thought I was ready. My presentation was well-received and I was bombarded by questions that indicated a strong interest level. I jumped around in my presentation to handle them as best I could, but never got back to finishing it. When my time was up, I was confident that I had covered all the major selling points and secured a follow-up meeting for the next month. As I was congratulating myself on the drive back to Manhattan, I realized I had left out the one thing my manager had told me was a real industry hot button: the on-site product sampling at the ski areas. I realized at that moment that I had memorized the words without really understanding the intent of what I was saying and losing sight of what I wanted. By memorizing the script in order, a simple change in order left me unprepared and almost cost me the sale.

1. **Take it off the page.** When you first read a script out loud, your goal is to try and connect to each line, or "take it off the page," as they say in acting. This is done by looking down, taking a breath, and getting the first line in your head before looking up

and saying it out loud on an exhale. Repeat this for each line. Do not worry about the timing or the exact phrasing, just go through the process and accept however it comes out.

2. **Avoid line readings.** Forget how you may have heard the script read by anyone else and don't predetermine how you're going to say a line or which words you are going to emphasize. Doing so leads to getting stuck in a pattern that sounds overly rehearsed and is very difficult to break. If you've ever seen a theatrical production more than once or been on a movie set, you'll notice that good actors rarely say their lines exactly the same way every time. If you're really being honest, focusing on the moment, and listening and responding to the other person, you *should* sound different each time. And because you are coming from a truthful place, each time will be just as compelling and powerful in its own way. Always leave room for variations in your speech and don't be married to a set line delivery. Think of the many ways Robert DeNiro famously improvised the line "You talkin' to me?" in *Taxi Driver*.

3. **Connect to the lines.** It's critical that you connect to the lines emotionally as well as intellectually. Repeat the lines aloud again and take notice of what emotions and thoughts they stir in you. Do you feel calm or excited, confident or silly? Especially note lines that offer imagery and paint pictures in your mind. Try to communicate those pictures and feelings with the words you are given. Also note lines where you feel uncomfortable or unsure, which will be further addressed in Step 5.

4. **Get physical.** If you're having trouble relating to the words, try writing them down in your own handwriting or making big gestures while you're speaking them. This act of physically connecting the words from our heads to our hands and seeing them in our own handwriting is not only a good way to familiarize ourselves with a script, but also helps us to personalize it and take ownership of the words.

5. **Speak out.** This technique is used to identify areas in the script in which the actor is uncomfortable or has not fully digested its meaning. As you read aloud, you also want to pay close attention to those places that trip you up. Poorly crafted sentences and unclear or vague statements are much more obvious when

we say them out loud, as opposed to reading them in our heads. Speaking out is a powerful tool for determining precisely what part of a script you are not connected with. You can be sure that if you are not connecting to it, neither will your client. It is critical to fully work this out *before* you get in front of your client.

How it works: The actor reads his script out loud, and when she comes across a line that she stumbles over or doesn't know why she's saying it, she simply "speaks out," or acknowledges it verbally. If the actor reads the following line: "To be or not to be? That is the question," she may feel awkward. Rather than moving on, she stops and speaks her feelings out loud: "I feel silly saying this. What am I really saying here? To be or not to be *what?*" Once she has acknowledged this problem by verbalizing it, she can start to address it by exploring it and talking through it. Once she is able to answer the questions to her satisfaction, she goes back to the script and continues rehearsing with a renewed sense of confidence in what she is saying.

Speaking out in sales

As a salesperson, how many times do you come across a line that is purposely vague, that does not ring true or feel authentic? Suppose you are reading your company presentation and you come across this line: *My product can help you reach your goals 50 percent faster than the competition.*

Stop. Ask yourself probing questions out loud, such as: "Is that really true? Where did that information come from? Is this in line with my client's goals? Do I even know what my client's goals are?" Determine what you need to do to resolve this. You may need to dig deeper into your script to see if the answer lies there. You may need to research the question within your company or industry. Or you may need more information from your client before you continue. Do not leave any line unexplored in your search for meaning and authenticity.

Reading at performance level

If you've followed the previous process, you should be fairly close to having your script committed to memory without consciously attempting to do so. You are now ready to practice a *real* delivery. I like to start with what's called an "over-the-top" read-through. Most people don't speak with as much energy or personality in business as they do in their personal lives—we tend to flatten things out, pull them in. In order to pump things up, it is helpful to go over the top, and then push yourself a bit further. (If you are one of those salespeople who is always percolating at a near-boil, please disregard this step.) Look at the following script and read it out loud with as much energy and excitement as you can muster. It's another opportunity to get your bad actor out.

Sample script

The Internet has become critical in reaching potential buyers. Studies show that buyers are 50 percent more likely to use the Internet than newspapers when they are searching for your product. As part of our full-service commitment, we offer you a targeted on-line marketing program to expose your company and your products to as many potential buyers as possible.

Now, keeping that energy up, read the same script aloud in your normal (indoor) voice. Because it's easier to "take it down" than bring it up, this is a great exercise to do before you go on a call (in your car or at home). It helps you retain some energy and personality while keeping it real.

If you find your delivery is getting stale or you're stuck (the words sound canned, flat, or monotone), try to say your script with the following variations:

☆ Eliminate the punctuation and mix up the cadences.

☆ Emphasize random words.

☆ Rap it or sing it.

☆ Say it while dancing, exercising, or moving around.

Writing your own script

Have you been thrown out on the street, armed with nothing but a brochure and a smile? Is your company script completely unsalvageable? No worries. Here are some steps for writing your own sales script.

1. **Talk it out.** Using a tape recorder, explain your product/service as if you were speaking to a friend who doesn't know a thing about your business. Don't assume anything is obvious. If you start at ground zero, you can always take away as necessary.

2. **Keep it conversational.** Write it down, but keep it conversational. Some of the best advice I ever got about writing was to write how I speak. In other words, don't get hung up on grammar and punctuation rules, as you'll notice in this book, sometimes you can break the rules to good effect. Sentence

fragments, for instance. And *never* ending a sentence with a preposition? Not something I believe in.

3. **Kill the buzz words.** Do you strategize, facilitate, or leverage? Good for you! Now write that in normal English. Buzz words and industry jargon cause eyes to glaze over, so why take a chance when you can easily say instead: I help, I teach, I show, I build. Always use the simplest, most precise words you can.

4. **Use a dramatic story arc.** Use the key elements of drama to build your story and create suspense. (This will be discussed in Chapter 7.)

Whether you're working with someone else's script or creating your own, it's important to trust the process. Most people (actors included) think they have to embellish what they say, or think they have to sound better than they usually do, adding emphasis in order to be heard and make their case. The fact is that when you are prepared, truthful, in the moment, and know what you are saying and why, you are well on your way to becoming a compelling presenter. Now that you have your presentation, you will learn how to deliver it with impact in Chapter 9.

EXERCISES

1. Use a script from your company or industry and answer the following questions: What is this script about? What is at stake for my client? What is my company trying to get across? How do I feel about it?

2. Circle any words or statements that are vague or make you uncomfortable.

3. For each sentence in the script, ask yourself: What am I really saying here? What do I want?

4. Research any areas about which you are still unclear. If you cannot find a satisfactory answer, rephrase it or throw it out.

5. Read your script aloud using the speaking out technique, stopping whenever you stumble or come across something that does not ring true. Review steps three and four of the rehearsal process before continuing.

THE DRAMA: UNCOVERING URGENCY

7

"I love acting. It is so much more real than life."

~Oscar Wilde

Mary and Adam sell airtime for competing local commercial television stations and each has Auto World as a client. When Mary meets with Craig, the owner of Auto World, she imparts a passion and belief that her station is the single most important tool Craig can use to increase his business. Mary takes Craig on a compelling journey starring the qualified, loyal, ready-to-buy consumer he can expect to reach with her station. Noting the heated battle between Auto World and their competitor, Car City, Mary builds her story up to a cliffhanger. Will customers turn to the superior service and value available at Auto World when they are ready to buy their next car? Or, will the opportunity be lost forever when the customer chooses to do business with Car City, all because Craig failed to get his message out over the airwaves of Mary's television station?

When Adam meets with Craig, he delivers a flawless presentation full of colorful charts and graphs. This presentation, he believes, proves that his television station reaches more qualified viewers each week than Mary's station. Adam pushes Auto World to close by reminding Craig that inventory is limited and rates are likely to increase by the end of the week.

Which salesperson won Craig's business?

Aren't we told as salespeople that it's our job to *create urgency* with the prospect? Contrary to common belief, I don't believe that urgency is something you can force upon another person. Urgency must exist within your prospects, and no matter how latent, it is our job to help them discover it so they can take the necessary actions. The urgency and motivation we discover within ourselves, as outlined in Chapter 5, can't help but rub off on prospects. However, without an equally strong need and desire within the buyer, it will be difficult to close a sale—and keep it closed. Indeed, some prospects may get caught up in *your* urgency, only to suffer buyer's remorse the next day after returning to their normal state.

An effective way to establish urgency comes straight out of drama. Admittedly, most sales situations are not the stuff of great drama. Few of us are selling African safaris or trips on a space shuttle. Still, drama can always be found in the smaller choices we make in our daily lives by discovering what's important, extraordinary, and significant in those individual decisions. In this chapter, you will learn how to find the drama within any sales situation in order to produce urgency within the buyer—no matter how well-hidden.

Acting techniques for finding the drama in sales:

☆ Create a dramatic selling journey.

☆ Discover the importance.

☆ Raise the stakes.

DRAMA AND SALESPEOPLE

When I combine the word *drama* with *sales*, do phony, pushy salespeople come to mind? When I mentioned to a sales manager in charge of dozens of salespeople for a large electronics chain that I was writing a book about acting techniques to help salespeople close more sales, he looked at me with skepticism. He said,"Julie, salespeople are dramatic enough." Though that may be true, in my experience, our flair for the dramatic is frequently misdirected. Have you ever seen a seller who's just lost a big account or received a charge back on a commission? Or how about a salesperson who finds the coffee machine empty? These are some Oscar-worthy performances! And yet, I've been with sellers on calls that are so dull and unmemorable that I have a hard time recalling what was discussed the next day. Imagine my surprise when I heard this same salesperson give a passionate account of the call to a co-worker with enough dramatic twists and turns to rival a Spielberg movie! Too often, sellers check their passion and their personalities at the client's door. Why should drama be reserved for only those closest to us when it can effectively be used to highlight the emotional and engaging aspects of a selling situation and trigger urgency within a buyer?

"The truth is not enough if it is neither dramatic nor interesting nor unique." ~ Michael Shurtleff, author of *Audition*.

Drama comes from a Greek word meaning "to do or "to act." Dictionary.com defines it as*: A situation or series of events that produce vivid, emotional, intense and even conflicting feelings, or is of striking interest.* Aren't the words *emotional, vivid,* and *of striking interest* words you'd love to have your client associate with you or your product or service?

Drama engages people; it draws them in. Characters have a dramatic purpose that we care about and can identify with on an intellectual and emotional level. They often have great challenges to overcome, allowing us to powerfully experience their journey. As salespeople, we can use the dynamics of a dramatic journey as well to engage our prospects and identify needs and urgency.

CREATING A DRAMATIC SELLING JOURNEY

"Drama is life with the dull bits cut out."~Alfred Hitchcock, director

In order to engage your prospect in a dramatic journey, identify the following five dramatic elements within the prospect's current situation:

1. Interest

We've all met that buyer who sits back, lets us go through our entire presentation, only to announce that she's "not really looking for anything right now," or her business is "just fine as it is." Have we met the one person in the world who has no needs or has all their needs and dreams fulfilled? I doubt it. Even in plot-less movies such as *Before Sunrise* or plays such as *Waiting for Godot*, the characters are still interested in something. It may not be readily apparent, or it may be disguised in circular conversations, but it is there if one looks hard enough.

People often lose sight of their own needs or the urgency of their situation when overwhelmed with a multitude of responsibilities and decisions. As salespeople, we are in a unique position to help our customers rediscover them by pointing out what is of striking interest and work toward a satisfying resolution.

2. Uncertainty

Even if we know that there will be a happy ending—the guy is going to get the girl, the client is going to buy our product—it's the element of uncertainty as to how the story and the solution will unfold that makes it dramatic. People are naturally curious and want to know how things turn out. A television series banks on that curiosity to keep viewers coming back week after week. Series such as *Lost* or movies that don't have a clear ending, such as *No Country for Old Men* or *Blade Runner*, leave a lot of viewers frustrated and wanting answers. Piquing the curiosity of a prospect by incorporating an element of uncertainty into your pitch or presentation can often get them to accompany you on the journey.

3. Emotion

People live for their dreams, hopes, and desires, not just practical solutions. How does what you sell play into that? Are you selling knives or are you selling the possibility of cooking like a great chef? Don't discount the often-intangible benefits that can capture your client's emotions.

4. Conflict

Though conflict is something most of us turn and run from, it is actually a key component of drama and can be used to move the sale forward. There are two types of conflict: external, such as the choice a prospect must make between you and your competitor, or internal, which exists within the prospect. Perhaps the prospect is struggling with the idea of making such a substantial purchase, even though it makes good sense. He may have some issues that he needs help resolving, or he may need to understand the consequences and risks of delaying his decision. Most people are uncomfortable with indecision. By acknowledging the conflict and offering a ready solution, you tap into that human desire to achieve resolution.

5. Action

The previous four conditions should culminate in compelling the prospect to take action in order to pursue an important goal and resolve a conflict or uncertainty.

An example of a prospect's dramatic journey

☆ Kelly needs to buy a car because her old one has finally died. She's put it off because she is able to ride the bus to work. However, her daughter will soon be going to a new school that does not provide bus service. (Interest)

☆ Kelly hasn't shopped for a car in years, so she doesn't have any idea what to look for or what she can afford. (Uncertainty)

☆ Kelly would love to have a new car that is not only practical and reliable, but also exudes an image of the success she aspires to within her company. (Emotion)

☆ Kelly has a friend who is an auto-broker as well as a neighbor who works at a nearby car dealership. She is not sure whether she should call either or both, and she doesn't want to feel obligated to purchase from them. (Conflict)

☆ Kelly decides to go to the nearest car dealership, as her daughter's school starts in a week and she is tired of agonizing about the decision. (Action)

Authentic Urgency.

There is a big difference between authentic urgency and the manufactured urgency of "I'm expecting an offer from another buyer today," or "Buy it now because the price goes up at five o'clock." People can spot false offers and concocted urgency miles away. The boy who always cries "wolf!" or the seller who always screams "fire sale!" will not be taken seriously.

In order to find authentic urgency within our client's situation, we can use two techniques that actors use to find the urgency within their character's circumstances: discovering importance and raising the stakes.

DISCOVERING THE IMPORTANCE

"The audience will not tune in to watch information. You wouldn't, I wouldn't. No one would or will. The audience will only tune in and stay tuned in to watch drama." ~ David Mamet, playwright

Would you sit through a well-acted, two-hour movie about someone making a decision of little or no consequence? *Russell Crowe must decide whether to buy the brown or the black shoes. What will he do?!* Yet as salespeople, how many of us have wasted a brilliant sales presentation on a prospect not emotionally invested in the outcome? Unless the prospect sees the decision as important and urgent, we're simply playing to an empty house. Sellers need to uncover what's important to the prospect *before* they can establish urgency.

Hot Buttons

When something is important to a person, it usually hits one of five common hot buttons. By asking yourself the following questions, you can start to identify which hot button is playing a role in your client's decision. This will allow you to target your pitch accordingly and greatly improve your chances of making a dramatic connection.

    ☆ **Self-esteem:** How does this decision help the prospect feel better about herself and/or her situation?

    ☆ **Pride:** How does this decision affect the prospect's feelings about himself in relation to others in his company, in his industry, or among his sphere?

☆ **Ambition:** How does this decision affect the prospect financially or status-wise?

☆ **Security:** How does this decision cause greater or lesser security in the prospect's business or personal life?

☆ **Relationships:** How does this decision affect personal or business relationships?

An example of targeting hot buttons

Tina sells medical benefits and enjoyed a strong friendship with the human resources director for a large company. She even used a quote from him in her own company's brochure. When Jerry was replaced with a new director, Wendy, Tina anticipated the continuation of that relationship. She showed Wendy her brochure and talked about the strength of the two companies' relationship. Tina was surprised when Wendy said she would not be influenced by the past or Jerry's recommendations. In fact, Wendy announced that she was bringing in several new firms to pitch their business. Thrown off a bit, Tina continued with her presentation, but only succeeded in getting Wendy to agree to a follow-up meeting before making her final decision.

Before her next meeting, Tina can determine which hot button most affects Wendy in this particular decision and tailor her presentation accordingly.

☆ **Pride.** Wendy clearly wants to make her own mark on the company as evidenced by refusing to give weight to the opinion of her predecessor, Jerry.

★ Solution: Tina can show support and respect for the new director's decision to formulate her own opinion and provide her with a compelling case to consider Tina's company on its own merit.

☆ **Ambition.** A good purchasing decision would obviously put Wendy in a more favorable status with her new superiors.

★ Solution: Tina can highlight a success story that Jerry, the former director, or another company achieved by using her company.

☆ **Relationships.** Wendy may want to establish a relationship on her own terms, and therefore, instead of being swayed by Tina's closeness with the former director, actually feels pressured by this. Think of how you feel when it is assumed that you are going to like someone based on another's opinion:

"Oh, you're going to love my friend, Don!" Don't you often think, "Don't be too sure."?

★ Solution: Tina can focus on establishing a relationship with Wendy just as she would with any new client.

Raising the Stakes

Another way to find authentic urgency is an acting technique called raising the stakes, which involves escalating the importance of any situation through a series of associations to build urgency. Movies show great examples of characters raising the stakes:

If the hero doesn't find the kidnapped victim by midnight, the villain will shoot her. If the villain shoots her, the bomb will explode. If the bomb explodes, the countries will go to war. We've all seen this movie, right? The risks keep getting bigger, but so does the payoff.

Here's an example of raising the stakes in sales: Suppose you're a real estate broker and your client is *considering* selling her home because she'd *like* to move to a bigger place now that the kids are growing up. Therefore she'll *try* putting it on the market at a price that you know will not sell.

Look at these words: *considering*, *trying*. Remember what drama means: to do or to act. Not much action or urgency to act in these words, are there? How do you get the prospect in a mindset where she's using strong action words such as *must*, *need*, *will*? You can raise the stakes by exploring the consequences, both positive and negative. Let's consider our real estate example. What are the consequences of *not* selling?

✰ The house sits on the market too long; it becomes stale; people start to think there's something wrong with it.

✰ Buyers assume that the sellers are desperate, therefore they make lower offers.

✰ The house doesn't sell.

This is a good start, but we can dig even deeper. Imagine that it is one year later, and your sellers suddenly have to move because of a new job or new school. What happens now?

✰ They will have to lower the price again in order to generate renewed interest.

✰ They will be limiting their ability to buy a bigger house because interest rates may have risen.

✫ There may be a glut of homes on the market, driving down the price further.

The net result: They lose money on the sale of their home (short sale), can't afford to purchase their larger dream home (downsize), and/or are forced to wait the market out indefinitely and turn down the new job (stuck).

Raising the stakes may seem like a chapter out of the worst-case scenario handbook, but in reality, don't these things happen all the time? We sit on the sidelines and miss the market. We're not sure whether we should spend a little more for the perfect house, but then it's gone. I still remember the one-of-a-kind leather jacket I walked away from in a little boutique in Florence, the perfect condo on the park that I waited too long to make a decision on, the center-row season tickets that I let expire. Everyone has experienced wanting something, not pulling the trigger, and regretting it. As salespeople, it is our responsibility to raise the potential consequences in order to help our prospects make a fully informed decision.

So the next time you're stuck in the sales spin cycle of indecision and procrastination with a prospect, look for the components of a dramatic journey to help you get out: interest, uncertainty, engagement, conflict, and urgency. Draw them out; explore them. It's a more certain way to engage your prospect—and as we all know, engagement is one step closer to a lasting commitment!

<u>CREATING URGENCY BY RAISING THE STAKES:</u>
<u>A SALES SCENE</u>

THE CAST

PAM: An independent public relations consultant.

THE SETTING

Pam recently left a large public relations agency to venture out on her own. While she enjoys the freedom, she was unprepared for the need to continually drum up new clients, as she was used to working with a steady pool of in-house clients. Potential clients agree that what she offers is of interest, but they don't see a burning need to have a PR firm on board until disaster strikes.

DIRECTOR'S SCENE NOTES

PAM

I have no trouble getting a meeting. They seem to be interested, they think it's a nice idea, but I can't get anyone to get off the fence and make a decision.

JH

So they think it's *interesting* and *nice*. What do you think about those words?

PAM

They're pretty bland, aren't they?

JH

Not exactly action-oriented, must-have kind of words.

PAM

Exactly. So how do I get them to that point?

JH

Give me your seven-second sales pitch.

PAM

I help companies build a unique and differentiated brand image by articulating and disseminating their message to target audiences and avoiding costly miscommunication by maximizing their exposure through strategic planning.

JH

First, get rid of the buzz words, such as *disseminate* and *strategic*. Try it again in plain English.

PAM

I help companies build a brand image by getting their message out to the right audiences and creating champions among their customers.

JH

Much better. Now tell me this: Under what possible circumstances would I be happy that I had your PR services?

PAM

If your company were launching a new product, you would need the right message articulating the right differentiation, and most importantly the customer benefit—why the customer should care.

JH

Can you expand on that?

PAM

The right product launch can make or break its success. A bland, me-too message will not work, while leveraging an experienced PR person will help you launch the product in a unique, timely fashion to the right audiences. A PR person will also know the right tools to use from social media, to traditional media, to unique events such as flash mobs. We can also help train spokespeople on this new message and product, develop internal communications' plans, and discuss any potential issues or crises that could occur.

JH

The downside of waiting would be getting lost in the shuffle or wasting a lot of money on the wrong messages or the wrong vehicles, right?

PAM

Yes.

JH

What's a typical product launch and how long does it last?

PAM

They're all different, depending on industry, product, distribution, and so on. But for the typical client—a mid-sized software manufacturer, for example—it might include a trade show launch, press tour with key trade media, and beta test samples to product reviewers.

JH

How would a company handle this without a PR professional on board?

PAM

Guaranteed they would miss opportunities. They might put the press release out at the wrong time, reach out to only a few media rather than sharing the news in a strategic way, or position the product too technically—using jargon rather than benefit-focused language.

JH

Now I'm starting to sense the urgency. How can you get this urgency into your sales pitch earlier and build on it until they see the serious consequences of not hiring you?

PAM

I could make a hypothetical example—or better, I could use an example of a company in their own industry who handled it professionally, and one that mishandled it on their own.

JH

Yes!

EXERCISES

1. Decide in which of the five hot buttons this decision most likely affects your prospect: self-esteem, security, relationships, ambition, or pride. You don't have to be a detective to know that the sexy car is probably a self-esteem or ambition issue and financial planning relates to security.

2. Brainstorm as many positive consequences as you can that would affect your client's hot button, as determined in exercise 1. Continue to raise the stakes from good, to better, to best.

3. Brainstorm the negative consequences as well, going from bad to worse.

4. Walk through the consequences of the decision using the components of a dramatic journey: interest, uncertainty, conflict, and emotion.

5. Use good, solid rationale and logic to help your prospect take the step that *they very likely already want to take* and avoid the negative consequences of procrastination.

THE SCENE PARTNER: BUILDING RAPPORT

8

"I think acting can bring you closer to yourself and help you understand other people."

~William Hurt

James and Arjun both own construction firms specializing in small to mid-sized residential renovation and remodeling. Carrie and Jeff have asked them both to come in and bid on adding an addition to their home. James meets with the prospects, and after a few moments of small talk about the weather asks to see the area they are looking to expand. He asks a few standard questions regarding price and expectations before launching into his pitch. Noticing that Carrie talks in a slow, monotone voice, and fresh out of an NLP training course, James adjusts his cadence and delivery to match hers, even though he is normally an energetic speaker. When James asks for their business, Carrie and Jeff tell him they will get back to him.

Before giving his presentation Arjun asks to be shown around the entire house. He stops at each room, commenting and asking Jeff and Carrie questions about something that appears to have significance to them such as a photo, a toy, a pet, or other items. Arjun maintains his natural enthusiasm and before starting his presentation, asks a few thoughtful questions based on the information he learned during the tour, drawing out and addressing Jeff and Carrie's real needs, wants, and concerns regarding the addition. When Arjun asks for the business, there is no hesitation on the part of the couple, and Arjun leaves with a signed contract.

All things being equal, buying decisions come down to a relationship between a buyer and a seller. And building rapport is a crucial first step in a business—or any type of—relationship. Without rapport, you are unlikely to get the appointment or convince prospects to open up about their needs, and unlikelier still to close them. Buying decisions are heavily influenced by emotions, and rapport allows emotions to develop in a trusted atmosphere. Rapport is even more important as the number of choices buyers have continues to increase. In this global economy, buyers can choose to work with any number of sellers, or they can choose to work with no one at all and do their purchasing on-line.

Like two actors cast as best friends who meet for the first time on opening night, you and your prospect are scene partners thrown together on the business stage. And your relationship with your scene partner, in theater or in sales, can make or break your performance. The need to quickly establish rapport is critical in both situations, but approached very differently. Sellers often jump in on a purely intellectual basis, asking the same old questions and hoping that something "clicks" with the prospect. Actors use their thoughts, feelings, and imaginations to understand their partner beyond a surface level in order to develop an authentic rapport that leads to a believable performance. You can easily learn to apply these techniques to sales to quickly establish rapport with a new prospect or build a stronger relationship with your existing clients.

Acting Techniques for Building Rapport

☆ Using results-oriented role-playing.

☆ Listening and asking rapport-building questions.

☆ Mastering the Magic If.

☆ Developing empathy and identification using The Magic If.

☆ Turning negative or neutral client relationships into positive ones through substitution.

WHAT IS RAPPORT?

Think of when you met someone with whom you instantly clicked. Rapport is something we do almost instinctively when we make a new friend. Dictionary.com defines rapport as *a sympathetic relationship or understanding, marked by harmony, conformity, accord, or affinity.* You'll recognize the hallmarks of rapport—listening, accepting, validating, and identifying—within your close relationships. These are generally effortless and flow from one to the other, not necessarily in a linear fashion. Unfortunately, the time pressures and codes of behavior we operate under in business often serve to stifle our natural tendencies where rapport is concerned. We don't have the luxury of weeks or months to establish a solid foundation for a relationship. As a result, we end up following intellectually based models as if we were dealing with an automaton instead of a fellow human being.

AUTHENTIC RAPPORT

To quickly establish rapport, many sales trainers encourage the use of systematic programs such as NLP, or neuro-linguistic programming, which is based on the premise that "people like people who are like us."[1] NLP was born in the 1970s, a product of a mathematician and a linguistics professor and made famous by Tony Robbins. Although there are many great things we can learn from NLP, I'm not sure a mathematician would be my first choice for advice on relationship-building.

Mirroring and matching are two popular techniques in NLP that are widely taught in sales training programs for quickly establishing rapport. Mirroring involves copying the other person's facial expression, eye movements, gestures, posture, and even the exact words they use.[2] If a person crosses his right leg, you cross your left; if he raises his left eyebrow, you raise your right, as if he was looking into a mirror. Matching involves aligning your breath, vocal cadence, and tone with the other person, just as James did in the example at the beginning of this chapter by slowing down his pace to match that of the seller.

DON'T MIME ME

NLP has always struck me as a grown-up version of copy cat. It brings back memories of being followed down the street by a mime that mimicked every move I made until I finally shook him by darting into a store. It is another example of a sales technique that focuses on making superficial changes without changing anything internally. Every instruction I've read on matching and mirroring comes with the cautionary warning: *Make sure the other person doesn't notice you're doing it!* I don't believe that tricking someone into thinking we are "just like them" can create the authentic rapport and trust necessary to build an honest and sustainable relationship.

Though techniques such as NLP offer valuable tools for helping us to understand the inner workings of others (modalities of learning, for example), I believe that people are a lot more perceptive than techniques like mirroring or matching give them credit for and that most of us know—either consciously or subconsciously—when others are forcing rapport by pretending to be our doppelganger. I'm sure I am not alone in my preference for working with someone who is not a bit like me but is authentic and empathetic, as opposed to someone who is focused on copying the way I blink and breathe.

REQUIREMENTS FOR RAPPORT

Real rapport requires a certain level of courage. To get to know other people, we have to allow them to get to know us. We have to let our guard down if we expect others to do the same.

"Most performers don't have that rapport with the audience. They aren't that honest." ~Sammy Davis, Jr.

By being authentic in our roles (as discussed in Chapter 2) we can be honest, open, and give our prospects an opportunity to identify, empathize, and trust. But although this may make the prospect more likely to open up, it is only half of the equation. In sales, we are typically the initiators in the relationship, and it is our responsibility to seek out areas of identification and ways to relate to the prospect in order to create a fertile ground for authentic rapport. Although "people like people who are like them," I believe that they are more likely to do business with people that like *and* understand them.

How to Quickly Establish Rapport.

The challenge in sales is how to establish rapport quickly. Think about your current clients. What do you know about them? Do you know their job duties or their buying habits? Where they like to go to lunch? That only puts you on par with every other salesperson. But what do you *really* know about them? Do you know what it's like to drive 40 miles to get to their office by 7 a.m. in order to connect with their East Coast customers and meet with their sales team while worrying about making next month's payroll? What about how they're going to cover their children's schooling or what's going to happen with their aging parents? Do you really know your clients?

Obviously we can't be BFF with every client and prospect, so we usually end up taking some short cuts: We make assumptions that our clients have the same issues and concerns as others in their industry, position, or socio-economic group: *She's my mother's generation so she's probably pretty conservative. He's a car dealer so he probably loves to haggle.* Or we rely on asking a standard series of questions with the hope that something will resonate or we will stumble upon something that provides us with useful insight. Though these may work some of the time, there are more reliable ways to accomplish this. Actors use a variety of methods to step into their character's shoes and see the world from their specific perspective rather than a generalized version of it.

But how do you understand clients' perspectives when you know very little about the clients? How can you possibly know what it's like to be in their shoes when all you have are some facts about their business and a few physical characteristics? It is helpful to look at how an actor comes to understand his character. One way to do this is through role-playing.

RESULTS-ORIENTED ROLE-PLAYING

In acting, role-playing is a rehearsal tool. It's an opportunity for the actor to "try on" different aspects of their character and build relationships with their scene partner—without judgment. Unfortunately, role-playing is still used ineffectively by many sales organizations as a test to judge sellers on their knowledge and performance.

Results-oriented role-playing is based on the acting model. It is an exercise for learning about our clients, and finding points of connection and how we can best address their needs. Take a look at the following example of successful role-playing in Hollywood and how that translates into role-playing in business:

Role-Playing in Hollywood

During rehearsals for *Kiss of the Spider Woman,* the lead actors, William Hurt and Raul Julia, were having trouble establishing a relationship; Hurt's character, a sensitive, flamboyant homosexual, shared little common ground with Raul Julia's homophobic revolutionary. To better understand each other's character, Hurt suggested they rehearse by switching roles. The performance resulted in an Oscar for both Hurt and the film.[3]

Role-Playing in Business

Aaron finds his client Cynthia's demands irrational and unattainable. Using the following five steps, Aaron prepares to role-play the part of Cynthia with a colleague and discovers what may be the real motivation behind her demands: a need to outperform her predecessor's achievements. Equipped with a newfound understanding of Cynthia's viewpoint, Aaron is able to address his client's concerns and close the sale.

5 Steps for Results-Oriented Role-Playing.

1. **Throw out pre-conceived ideas.** Avoid broad generalizations about your client or prospect. Remember: They are three-dimensional human beings with *real* feelings, thoughts, and desires. Assumptions often keep you from seeing prospects for the unique individuals that they are.

2. **Describe your client's given circumstances.** If you are open-minded and non-judgmental, you will make observations and ask questions that are not colored by your assumptions, allowing you to paint a more accurate picture of who they are and what they want.

3. **Step into your client's shoes with the Magic If.** This valuable acting technique will be described in greater detail and will change the way you see your clients for good. The preparation you've done in the previous steps will prepare you for jumping

into your client's role by asking yourself: *"What would I do if I were really in this situation? Given these circumstances, what do I hope to achieve? What might I like to hear from a salesperson?"*

4. **Identify with your client.** Take everything you know about your client—personally and professionally—and find areas where you intersect. Do you share strong family values? A financial pressure to perform? A need to be right?

5. **Forget what you know about your product/service.** That's right. Forget it. Business owners and buyers alike are deluged with facts and figures from dozens—maybe hundreds—of salespeople. Put aside all the numbers, the percentages, the market shares, and start with a blank slate. Even if your client knows more than a little about your product, service, or industry, it will help you to see your presentation through your client's eyes.

Let's take a closer look at the acting-related steps in the role-playing process.

DESCRIBE YOUR CLIENT'S GIVEN CIRCUMSTANCES

In order to enter the character's world and appreciate his actions and choices, the actor must investigate the character's "given circumstances," typically the *who, what, where, when,* and *how* that the author has provided in the play or script. Often an actor is provided with a detailed description of his character, but sometimes an actor has just as little information to work with as we have about a new prospect. For example, here is Tennessee Williams's description of Stanley Kowalski in *A Streetcar Named Desire:*

Twenty-eight or thirty years old, roughly dressed in blue denim work clothes. Stanley carries his bowling jacket and a red-stained package from a butcher's.[4]

That's it! These two meager sentences tell you his age, that he works with his hands, that he likes to bowl, and that he buys and eats meat. From this, an iconic character is born. The great Marlon Brando took this small description and made it hard to imagine Stanley Kowalski being played any other way. Just like an actor taking on a role, we must be a detective and step into the world of our prospects in order to understand them better.

We may think we know only the very rudimentary facts of our prospects' circumstances—company, position, responsibilities, physical characteristics— but if we keep our ears and eyes open, we may be able to ascertain clues about their personal or family life, hobbies, interests, religious or spiritual beliefs, moral code, and so on. The more specific the better. Of course, the easiest way to get to know a potential client's given circumstances is to ask questions.

RAPPORT-BUILDING QUESTIONS

The type of questions we ask our clients or prospects is critical, not only in discovering their given circumstances, but also in creating rapport. Ask a personal question too soon, and you will put off the less-forthcoming prospect; beat around the bush, and you will try the patience of a busy one. Here are some guidelines for asking questions that will lead to thoughtful answers while establishing rapport.

1. Ask clarifying questions.

Remember the casting director's rule in Chapter 1: Don't ask general questions that require prospects to explain their business or industry to you. Imagine for a moment having to answer that routine question every time a salesperson called you—no wonder prospects grow impatient! Instead, ask clarifying questions that help you gain more insight into their jobs and the challenges they face. This will not only help you tailor your presentation or guide your line of questioning, but also demonstrate that you have taken the time to learn about their company.

2. Ask open-ended questions.

Questions that start with words such as *who*, *where*, *what*, *when*, *how*, and *why* require the prospect to respond with more than a simple yes or no and provide us with more helpful information.

3. Ask hypothetical questions.

Questions such as "What if…" or "Suppose that…" allow you to test the waters with ideas that the prospect may otherwise feel uncomfortable answering.

4. Rephrase their answer in a question.

Questions that reflect back to the clients' answers, such as "So you are concerned about the potential maintenance costs?" validate your prospects by acknowledging that you hear them. They will also indicate very quickly whether you have misinterpreted them.

Armed with this information, we are now ready to proceed to the next step, The Magic If:

THE MAGIC IF

"I'm curious about other people. That's the essence of my acting. I'm interested in what it would be like to be you." ~Meryl Streep

As an actor, how do you play a murderer with any kind of authenticity if you've never murdered? How do you play a lottery winner if you've never even bought a lottery ticket? The "Magic If" is a famous technique introduced by Stanislavski that helps actors relate to the often completely unrelatable lives of their characters.[5] The Magic If invites us to use our imaginations to transcend our own circumstances and step into those of another. In other words, *If everything around me were true, how would I behave?* We are all familiar with ideas from our childhood, such as: *What if I could fly? What if I were a princess?* It is only as adults that we learn to curb our imagination, but by exploring the answers to the question "What if?" we begin to truthfully discover how we—and in turn others—might think, feel, and act within their particular circumstances. The Magic If is really about identifying or empathizing with our client or prospect. Empathy is the ability to *identify with or vicariously experience the feelings, thoughts, or attitudes of another,* according to Dictionary.com.

Once we have explored our prospect's given circumstances and "tried them on" for size we are ready to identify with them.

IDENTIFYING WITH OUR CLIENTS

The ability to understand another on an emotional level is a powerful skill, as many buying decisions are based on or at least influenced by our emotions. Unfortunately, many of us get stuck identifying solely on an intellectual level. We get entangled in a process that never gets from our heads to our hearts, causing a big surprise when clients make choices that don't seem to make sense based on the facts. So how do we get in touch with the deeper emotions or feelings that may be driving another's actions?

In order to identify, we look at what emotions or experiences that we may have had that are, to some degree, like those our prospect is experiencing. Emotions or feelings are largely accessed by the subconscious and cannot be forced. If you've ever tried to cry on demand, you know what I mean. However, Stanislavski discovered that if the actor goes at it indirectly by focusing his attention on the character's circumstances until he believes in their possibility, the emotions and feelings may spontaneously grow within the actor.[6]

If we can get even a small sense of what the other person is feeling or experiencing, we are well on our way to developing empathy and identifying with our clients. This gives us a much better chance of establishing rapport and asking the types of questions that will help to unearth their needs.

APPLYING THE MAGIC IF IN SALES

Let's put the Magic If into practice with Eileen Jones, a buyer for an international shipping company.

Given Circumstances

Eileen has been with the company for 10 years. The company has been family-run for 70 years and Eileen's direct manager is one of the founder's grandsons. The company has been going through a downsizing and Eileen is responsible for reducing shipping costs. Despite the casual atmosphere, Eileen is always very professionally dressed, except for her shoes, which are plain, flat, and well-worn. In her mid-40s and single, she does not smile easily, her forehead is often furrowed, and her eyes tend to drift toward her computer and phone when meeting with her.

Apply the Magic If

We begin by asking ourselves questions such as: *What If I were a 40-year-old single woman working at a family-owned company that is struggling to stay profitable in a competitive market?* Then we explore the answers to this by delving deeper, asking ourselves more probing questions, such as: *Do I feel like an outsider in a family-run business? Would I be concerned about my job? Why do I keep up with fashion in an environment where it is clearly not important? Do I wish to be treated with more respect or do I aspire to greater responsibility? My shoes are incongruent with the overall care I take with my appearance: Did I walk a long way to catch the bus and get slammed with work as soon as I walked in the front door, leaving me no time to change my shoes? Do I have foot problems? Why am I always eyeing my computer with a furrowed brow? Am I expecting some bad news? What are my hopes for the day ahead as I ride the bus? Am I dreading the cuts I have to make in the budget? Am I looking forward to meeting with a salesperson today or is it just one more person trying to squeeze money out of a shrinking budget? What would be wonderful today?*

Look for identification

After fully exploring Eileen's circumstances, we should have a better understanding of her situation and what she is up against. But in order to bring this from merely an intellectual idea to an emotional feeling, we must look for something in our circumstances or experience that will help us identify with Eileen's circumstances. Perhaps Eileen's tenuous position in the company calls to mind moving into your first apartment shortly after purchasing a new car, only to receive news that your company was being bought by a competitor and layoffs were likely. As you struggled to stay positive and prove that you were a vital member of the team, the ever-present fear of being laid off drew closer.

Now, based on what you've discovered through the Magic If, you are better prepared to ask Eileen targeted questions that will not only help address her needs, but create rapport, questions such as "What does this down-sizing mean for you and how can I help?" or "What if I could show you how you can maximize your budget and save time with a couple of small changes to your existing plan?"

Ultimately, the more we *feel,* as opposed to *know,* what it's like to walk in our customer's shoes or sit in our prospect's chair, the more likely we are to establish authentic rapport, the more on target our questions and solutions will be, and the easier the subsequent steps in the sales process will be.

SUBSTITUTION

That client just doesn't get it. We don't get along. He's mean. She won't listen. Oh, if we could only work with people we like, what a wonderful world it would be. But in real life, this is rarely the case. Many times we are called upon to deal with difficult people, bullheaded people, even, dare I say, unlikable people. Do we give up and throw the possibility of establishing rapport, much less a relationship, out the window? Do we pawn them off on the eager new hire, or do we keep plying them with the same techniques that usually work with everyone else and hope they come to their senses? None of these is really effective.

Fortunately, there is a technique taught in many acting schools that can help smooth out your dealings with even the most difficult clients, called substitution.[7] Substitution is mentally replacing a negative or neutral person with a positive one. Though it doesn't change the other person, it does alter our attitude and actions, stimulate an emotional connection, and help build momentum for closing. Substitution can change the whole dynamic of a troubled or potentially toxic relationship.

Here's how it works. Say you were in a play and it called for you to be in love with your fellow actor. Let's also say that in reality, you can't stand that person. What would you do? You could fake it—like Richard Gere and Debra Winger purportedly had to do in *An Officer and a Gentleman*.[8] But odds are that you're not Richard Gere or Debra Winger. An easier way (and perhaps the way these stars managed it) is to look at your scene partner and focus on something about that person, some characteristic or attribute (eyes, lips, blue sweater) that reminds you of someone you actually *do* love. By concentrating on these specific attributes and substituting your scene partner for the person you love in your mind's eye, you are able to achieve the desired attitude and react more positively toward that person.

Substitutions work for any number of situations where you are simply "not feeling the love," whether it's a client, co-worker, or boss. You can quite literally substitute anyone for whom you have the feelings that you desire to re-create for them. You may look at your intimidating boss and see the sweet face of your basset hound and suddenly find yourself feeling a little less frightened and perhaps even slightly amused. You may be sitting across from your client and smell the aftershave of a beloved uncle, and feel a greater sense of connection. Substitution allows us to exchange our negative feelings about a person or situation for positive ones and in so doing, discover new more effective ways to communicate and work through road blocks.

Using Substitution in Sales

While selling radio advertising during the 1990s for a new adult contemporary station in Denver, I was assigned to Denise, a buyer for a large advertising agency who had a history of bringing more than one salesperson to tears. She was tough to get in to see and even tougher once you were actually in front of her. Denise had a sharp East Coast "get to the point" attitude and was not shy about prodding you along or cutting you off if you took too long getting there. But she controlled a substantial budget for several major clients, so there was no going around her without the risk of being removed from the account and blacklisting the station from receiving any future business.

When I finally got a meeting with Denise, I was understandably apprehensive. What if she didn't like me? What if she attacked me personally, as she'd done to a former colleague of mine? I tried to think if there was anything about her that reminded me of someone more pleasant and less intimidating. There was something about her voice that seemed familiar to me when I called to make the appointment. She had a rough voice, speaking in short and abrupt sentences through a heavy Brooklyn accent, and I knew her to be a lifelong smoker. Upon reflection, I realized that Denise's voice reminded me of my favorite aunt. Aunt Lucy also came across very gruff but was really a marshmallow. Underneath her tough exterior was a big heart and a razor-sharp sense of humor that I grew to love. I decided to concentrate on my client's voice and imagine my aunt in my mind's eye and see where this would lead me.

When I entered her office, Denise was on the phone, making no acknowledgment of my presence for a good two minutes. Normally this would intimidate me, but instead I grabbed a chair and pulled it up to her desk. As I waited for Denise to finish, I listened to her familiar gruff voice and felt a smile come to my face as I imagined waiting for my aunt to get off the phone so I could talk to her. When she got off, she peered at me from over the top of her glasses: "So what have you got?" Obviously rapport-building questions were literally out of the question. I paused as I imagined hearing my aunt ask that question, and with a genuine smile was able to reply, "Well, I think you're going to be pleasantly surprised." As I launched into my pitch, Denise was exactly as advertised: abrupt, full of interjections and objections, but *I* was different: I was able to laugh and take each counter-point with good humor and turn it into a positive. Soon she visibly lightened up and I asked her if she would like to continue the discussion over lunch. She scoffed and said "I only have lunch with people I've worked with for a while." I laughed, "You're going to be stuck working with me for a while so we may as well get to know each other." We had a lunch date set for the next week and I had an order before then.

When deciding who to use as a substitution, consider who brings up the feelings or attitude that will best help you with your prospect: a high school friend you haven't seen in years, a favorite teacher, a kind but cantankerous uncle. Look for certain qualities that make you feel comfortable and positive. Does the way your client squints his eyes while he's listening to you remind you of an old professor? Does the prospect's jacket bring back memories of your first boss?

Employing substitution requires a certain amount of concentration and relaxation, which you will have already done in your pre-call preparation (Chapter 4). Don't imagine that you will ever forget who you are talking to or what your real circumstances are. Substitution is simply a springboard into a new relationship dynamic. Keep in mind that although you will be initially focusing on the substitution to help adjust your attitude, eventually you will be creating a relationship with the person in front of you and not need to use it any longer.

<u>A SALES PRO SCENE</u>

THE CAST

KEN: The owner of a commercial cleaning business.
BARBARA: The new manager of a multi-location business.
LINDSAY: Ken's wife.

THE SETTING

Ken currently does the cleaning for a number of single-lo-
cation clients, but has determined that the key to expanding his business in the future is to win a contract with
a large company with multiple locations. After several
attempts, he finally set a meeting with Barbara, the busy
new manager of one of these key companies he has targeted.

<u>DIRECTOR'S SCENE NOTES:</u>

JH
How did you get an appointment with Barbara?

KEN
I called her half a dozen times and told her I could do a
better job for her than the company they've been working
with for the past five years, but she was always too busy
to see me, so I finally stopped by. I think I put her on the
spot. She wasn't particularly friendly.

JH
Tell me what you know about her and her circumstances.

KEN
She's probably in her mid 20s. She was a manager at one of
their offices and three months ago she was put in charge of
operations for the whole company. She's actually pretty
young for that position. She must work very hard because
she's always out at one of their locations, and I know she
gets into the office at seven.

JH

So, let's try a little Magic If on Barbara. What if you were at your first job out of college and suddenly promoted to a position with all kinds of new responsibilities and relationships? And what if you had more people wanting to meet with you than you had time for, because they all knew that they had a new opportunity to sell their products now that the old regime was gone? If you were in that position, how would you feel about meeting with a new, unproven cleaning service when you have no reason to think the old one is broken?

KEN

I guess that would be pretty far down my list of priorities.

JH

What specifically might you be feeling?

KEN

I'd be feeling pressured and annoyed.

JH

Can you identify any experiences where you have felt pressured into doing something you felt was relatively insignificant at the time?

KEN

I had just taken out a loan on the business so we could expand, bought a bunch of new equipment and vans, and my wife, Lindsay, decided we needed to renovate our kitchen. I kept putting her off because I really didn't think it was necessary—and certainly not when I had all these other priorities.

JH

So what happened?

KEN

Let's just say I have a new kitchen.

JH

But if it wasn't a priority, how did Lindsay convince you to do it?

KEN

She reminded me that as part of our expansion we were going to be doing a lot more entertaining. She went through everything that was wrong with the current kitchen and really made me see what impression it would give people coming into our home for the first time. People we were asking to invest money with us. Lindsay laid out all the costs and timing for the renovation so that I didn't have to be involved in any of the decisions or details. It made me realize that I needed to take care of some very basic things at home as well as the big picture at work.

JH

Excellent example! Now how could you apply that to your meeting with Barbara?

KEN

I could make a detailed list of everything that needs improvement in all of their offices and how we would address it. And I would stress that while it may seem insignificant, it is all the little things that add up to making a first impression—which is really important in the big picture.

JH

Great plan. Let me know how it works!

EXERCISES

1. Select one client that you are having trouble establishing rapport with and describe his or her given circumstances.

2. Ask yourself: "What If I were in these circumstances?" Continue to probe using the situation, your imagination, and your intuition.

3. Identify a similar experience or situation from your own life and note what feelings it brings up and how this changes what questions you will ask your client.

4. Select someone in your life that you have a positive relationship with and mentally substitute that person for your difficult client. Note how this change affects your attitude and behavior with this client.

5. Dedicate one week strictly to establishing rapport with your existing clients as well as new prospects, and note how this affects your working relationship during the next month.

ACT III:
The Performance

THE OPENING NIGHT: TAKING COMMAND OF THE STAGE

9

"We are born at the rise of the curtain and we die with its fall…and of what use is it to say to audience or to critic, 'Ah, but you should have seen me last Tuesday?'"

~Micheal Macliammoir, famous Irish actor

Kevin sells highly specialized medical equipment that collects and separates whole blood into its components used for surgery and treating various diseases. The size of the necessary investment and the complexity of the machines means he must make his presentation first to a team of nurse operators who will be using the product, and then to a small group of hospital executives who will be making the financial decision. Kevin is confident and engaging as he demonstrates his product to the nursing staff. But once Kevin gets into the boardroom to discuss benefits and financial value with the executive decision-makers, he is stiff and formal. His arms are either folded behind his back or buried in his pockets as he rocks back and forth on his feet. Kevin's voice is strong and clear, but his delivery lacks variety. One sentence quickly blends into the next.

Twenty minutes into his presentation, his audience begins to fade. At this point, Kevin realizes he has not moved, at all. Thinking perhaps he should, he begins to pace. Although this regains the attention of the group, they are now confused. His movements do not seem to have a purpose or to correspond with what he's saying. Afterward, during the question period, it is obvious that the group did not comprehend much of the information Kevin delivered, and the crucial first steps in the decision-making process suffered. The team is unclear about the equipment's benefits, and another meeting is required to clarify.

Each presentation is a new beginning—an opening night, if you will. A performance, whether on the theater or business stage, is a temporal and fleeting thing. Yet, it can leave a vivid impression on your audience long after you have exited that stage. The client or group you're in front of today did not see your flawless, passionate performance of yesterday. They can judge you only on the present. So how do you consistently deliver a fresh, powerful performance day after day, client after client? Just as an actor learns to re-create the magic night after night, audience after audience, you can also learn to deliver a confident, compelling presentation each time by using proven acting techniques to take command of the business stage.

Acting techniques for taking command of the business stage:

☆ Communicating with intention.

☆ Speaking with animation.

☆ Giving nonverbal cues.

☆ Adding vocal variety.

TAKE COMMAND OF THE STAGE

The first time I stepped onto the stage, I was overcome with fear and self-consciousness. "Take command of the stage!" the director shouted. "Own the spotlight!" I immediately proceeded to make my actions bigger and more dramatic. I moved about at random, bouncing from one side of the stage to the other. I practically shouted my lines and over-emphasized every other word. As you can guess, this is not what he meant. It took me months to understand his direction, but it doesn't have to take you that long. In order to grab the audience's attention and get them to *buy into* the "reality" of your role, your business, or your product, you have to inhabit your space with complete conviction and confidence. With the same techniques I used to *command the stage*, I started winning more business, breaking sales records, and presenting confidently to Fortune 500 companies.

COMMUNICATING WITH INTENTION

By this point, you will have clarified your intentions (Chapter 5) and become clear about what you are saying and why (Chapter 6), but somewhere between your thoughts and the recipient's brain, the message may be getting diluted, miscommunicated, or not expressed at all. Perhaps your voice is hard to follow, your words imprecise, your body language distracting, or you display a lack of conviction. Relying on your words to do all of your selling is a quick route to being out-sold.

Actors need to be experts at effective communication. They know that communication is based on the need to be heard by their partners, typically in the hopes that it will impact their feelings, attitude, or behavior. It is more than just sending out words; it is sending out feelings as well. As sellers, we need to remember that communication is a circle, not a straight line. It is not enough to *feel* as if you're communicating if your prospect doesn't receive it, or misinterprets it, or is not compelled to act on it. The intention of our words needs to be supported by our physical presence. Just as we should always be reading our recipients for nonverbal cues (addressed in detail in the next chapter), they are reading us for cues as well. Prospects get confused, or worse, suspicious when our body language is not congruent with our words. So how do we make sure that our outsides match our insides? Let's take a closer look at the elements that make up our physical delivery and how an actor approaches each.

SPEAKING WITH ANIMATION

No, I don't mean talking like a cartoon character. I am referring to the pre-Disney dictionary definition of animated: *full of life, vivacity, and spirit*. Uta Hagen defines animated talking as having our words literally "spring from us, from our body, mind, and soul, with spontaneity, urgency, and inevitability."[1] Much of the motivation to speak will come from the work we've done in previous chapters. In order for the words to "spring from our body, mind and soul" with "urgency," as Ms. Hagen suggests, our need to talk must come from three core beliefs:

1. We have something important to say.

2. We must say it now.

3. We must be the ones to say it.

If you are unsure or vague about any of these beliefs, your delivery will lack commitment, passion, and urgency. Review chapters 5 and 6 to determine how to strengthen your beliefs and thus, your delivery.

GIVING NONVERBAL CUES

What percentage of effective communication is based on our spoken words? Would you guess 25, 50, 80 percent? Wrong! How about this: a whopping *7 percent!* Studies say that 55 percent of communication is visual (body language, expression, eye contact), 38 percent is vocal (pitch, speed, volume, tone), and only 7 percent comes from our words.[2] Though it is hard to believe that you could sell your product or service without saying a single word, as this study seems to imply, it does suggest that your body language could easily make or break a sale.

Self-Consciousness

Have you ever been on the receiving side of a presentation where the salesperson looked so uncomfortable in his body that it made you feel uncomfortable? Actors can feel awkward on a stage if they do not have a physical destination. As we discussed in Chapter 3, we are always coming from somewhere and going somewhere. Every move we make, from scratching our nose to sitting down in a chair, is part of a logical purpose. Without a physical destination or motivation, a sense of self-consciousness and panic can overcome an actor or a seller and lead to a poor performance. How do we handle this? Well, many react just like Kevin did in the boardroom, falling back on subconscious movements, such as rocking back and forth, or folding and unfolding our arms. Or we start adopting what we assume are "natural" positions—which suddenly feel anything *but* natural! The problem is that we haven't made communication a *physical activity* as well as a mental one, and our movements have no real justification.

As salespeople, we have to be present, both mentally and physically, in order to communicate at our fullest. An actor doesn't just randomly wander across the stage; she has a purpose for every move. A speaker who ping-pongs from one side of the room to the other is distracting and hard to follow. Fortunately, if you are warmed up, your body will be loose and free, and more likely to naturally fall in line with your intentions. That's why the warm-ups in Chapter 4 are so important, as are the setting of objectives in Chapter 5. This singleness of purpose, to communicate our message effectively, helps to relieve some of that self-consciousness and make your delivery much more impactful.

Stage Blocking

Often, an actor is given very specific actions to take during a scene, such as cross to the couch on this line, pick up a glass on that cue, turn off the lights when the phone rings. If these directions are not logical to the actor, they will not only feel awkward and forced, but look that way as well. Famous director Arthur Hopkins said: "The reason for walking is destination!"[3] We don't walk to break up the monotony or because we've been standing in one spot for too long, as Kevin did in his presentation. We walk to get somewhere: to the whiteboard to write down a key point, toward the audience to get a closer look at their reaction, to the podium to reference our notes. Although there's no need to have every move blocked out as the actor might, you still need to know *why* you are moving and *where* you are going. I am not suggesting you stand stock still either, but that you create a reason that is logical to you to get you moving in a natural way with a purpose.

Gestures

What do I do with my hands? This is a common problem that plagues actors, speakers, and salespeople alike. Should you leave them hanging at your sides? Placed behind your back? Politely crossed in front of you? Gestures and movements can support what you're saying, emphasize key points, and provide visual variety. They can also be distracting and off-putting. Here are some tips on using gestures to your advantage:

☆ Don't gesture just to gesture. As your words and movements do, your gestures are carrying out an intention—to drive home a point, or illustrate an example. Every gesture should be connected to a thought and not just externally added on without justification.

☆ Look for places to include gestures. For example, if you are demonstrating an action (tossing, ducking, or weaving), describing a person or a thing (he was *this tall,* or it went from *here to there*), or making a key point (*this is why the extra coverage makes sense*).

☆ Make your gestures a natural part of your presentation by rehearsing with them.

☆ Review the physical warm-up section in Chapter 4 in particular. Focus on moving your body around freely while you speak.

Repetitive gestures

If overused or odd, gestures can look robotic and distract your listener. If someone makes a repetitive movement while she's speaking, our focus is drawn to the movement, not the message. Do you remember Bill Clinton's signature gesture? The loosely closed fist that would go up and down emphasizing everything he said? Though it didn't seem to hurt his career, on most of us it would appear to be simply a technique and therefore forced.

The eyes have it.

The eyes don't lie. If you say one thing and mean another, your eyes will give you away and your more perceptive prospects will pick it up. That's why so many presentation training classes that rely on fixing only our external gestures aren't as effective as fully integrating physical change with the mind and thought process. If you are completely aligned with your message, your eyes will enhance your performance by reinforcing your belief in your product or company, your genuine interest in your prospects, and your confidence in your ability to help them.

Try this exercise. Look in the mirror, and, without saying a word or forcing a change in your expression, think about a past disappointment you experienced. Notice your eyes. Can you see the disappointment in them? Now try congratulating yourself on a job well done, again, without saying a word. Isn't that readable in your eyes as well? We make sure our eyes are speaking the truth by making sure we are clear about our message, and our intentions are focused on the client, rather than ourselves.

A note about eye contact: Though eye contact is important, relentless staring at your listener will not only create discomfort, but can also cause you to forget your words. Remember that it is natural to look away when thinking about something; just don't drift away too long. Always bring yourself back to your prospect.

A Radiant Smile

We all know the power of a genuine smile. We've been told that even a phony smile has the power to change our mood. I've experienced that myself. But if you're relying on a fake smile to get you through a sales call or presentation, be forewarned: You are very likely to be found out. A real smile uses many involuntary muscles around your mouth, cheeks, foreheads, and eyes, whereas a forced or polite smile uses only the outer muscles around the mouth and is therefore easier to spot. But a real smile can be seen in the eyes. Try it yourself in the mirror. Think of something that really makes you smile, such as your lover, your wife or husband, your kids, your dog, or closing a big sale. Now, think of something that makes you unhappy and force yourself to smile. Ask yourself honestly: Would you invest money in the person with the phony smile staring back at you? If you've done a proper warm-up, prepared a positive "Moment Before," and clarified your motivation and intentions, you shouldn't have to fake your smile.

"Smalking"

I was recently introduced to this great word—which you won't find in any dictionary—by Louise, a development associate at a local PBS station. She uses the word *smalking* to describe the act of smiling while talking, and she is an expert at it. It's an engaging and rare skill. I challenge you to look around and count the number of people who you come in contact with today who actually smile when they speak and notice how it draws you in. Contagious, isn't it? For those who do "smalk," it probably comes very easily. For the rest of us, it may require a little more concentration, the way simultaneously rubbing your stomach and patting your head does. But it can be done. When you find yourself smiling, try slowly extending it while you are talking for just a few seconds at a time. Keep doing this until you can hold it longer and it becomes more natural to you. Like anything new you take on, it may seem a bit forced and unnatural at first, but with practice, you may be able to incorporate it into your communication style with ease.

VOCAL VARIETY

Your voice can help or hurt your presentation. Remember: 38 percent of what we communicate is derived through the quality of our voice, not the actual words. It's hard for anyone to listen to someone speak for more than a few minutes without his or her mind wandering. A droning voice will get people wandering even quicker. Your pitch, pace, and volume all play a crucial part in grabbing and holding a listener's attention, being heard, and even more importantly, being remembered. Do you pause for emphasis, modulate up and down for variety, or alternate between fast and slow to make an important point? Here are just a few of the ways to add vocal variety to your speech.

Pitch

Think of your voice as floating on a scale. Are you using only the middle C? Or are you playing other keys as well? A good place to change pitch is when you want to emphasize a word or make a point. "Imagine if you could *save five hundred dollars every year* just by flipping this switch?" Your words start to come alive when you vary your pitch and tone, but make sure your choices are logical. Don't just mix it up at random, such as ending sentences on an up note like a question, or emphasizing irrelevant words. This can confuse your listener.

Pace

We all have our own rate of speech, and if we try to change it to match every client or prospect we meet (as matching and mirroring techniques suggest), we will end up focusing more on our new speech pattern than our message. However, speeding up or slowing down when we want to make a major point or build to a dramatic climax is an extremely effective way to engage the listener.

Never rush through a presentation because of outside pressure, as this will significantly drain it of its impact. If a client makes you feel like you are on borrowed time, focus on making only one or two key points, or ask if you can reschedule.

Volume

If you have the opportunity to speak, it's a shame to throw it away by not being heard. I've had to strain to hear many presentations where the presenter was not even aware he or she was hard to hear or understand. Don't assume you know the volume of your voice. Take someone along with you on an appointment and get feedback. If you are asked even once to repeat something, you need to speak louder than you think is normal. Most people, when asked to speak up or repeat something, simply talk louder for a few seconds before reverting back to their normal volume. Often, the listener won't ask again because he or she is uncomfortable, so be sure and keep your volume elevated for the remainder of the presentation. If you are a naturally soft speaker, work on talking louder than is comfortable throughout your day. This way it won't feel so unnatural to you when you do it in a sales call.

In addition to making sure we are heard, raising and lowering your volume can add anticipation and excitement to your presentation. Raising it forces attention, just as lowering your voice to a dramatic stage whisper lets a listener know something important is being said, or that he is being let in on a secret. Just be wary of overusing this tool, because a little goes a long way.

Pauses

A well-placed pause before a key statement can let the listener know you are saying something of importance, and a dramatic pause afterward allows the impact of what you said to sink in. As noted earlier, casting directors like to see actors pause before responding—and so do prospects and clients. It lets them know that you're thinking and taking in their words.

THE ABCS OF THE 10-MINUTE STRETCH

No matter how compelling a speaker or presenter you are, the typical listener's attention will wane after about 10 minutes.[4] By planning to shake things up every 10 minutes, you can be assured of re-engaging them. In addition to making sure your listeners continue to pay attention, it will reenergize you as well. Try breaking things up with one of the ABC's every 10 minutes during your presentation.

A. Ask questions.

B. Bring out a prop.

C. Create your style or movement.

Pre-presentation checklist:

1. Have you created a "Moment Before" that will jump start you into your presentation on a positive and energized note? (Chapter 3)

2. Have you warmed up your body so you are free to be physically and vocally expressive? (Chapter 4)

3. Have you clarified what your intentions are for this presentation? (Chapter 5)

4. Have you broken down your script and defined what you are saying and why you are saying it? (Chapter 6)

VIDEOTAPING

Although many salespeople cringe at the idea of being on camera, videotaping yourself is an excellent way to see whether what you are feeling or thinking is being communicated effectively. People used to tell me that I looked very serious when in fact I wasn't necessarily feeling that way. I shrugged off their comments until I saw myself on camera, and guess what? They were right! I was surprised to discover that, often, while I thought I was smiling, the message had apparently not gotten from my brain to my face. I think most of us have a default expression without being aware of it. I have to work at making sure the muscles in my face and mouth are relaxed, and that my intentions are focused not only on imparting information, but enjoying the process as well.

Videotaping yourself is an excellent way to find out what reflexive gesture, expression, or action you might be making that is not serving your intentions. Seeing yourself on tape is sometimes a bit of a shock, but remember: It's only news to you—the rest of the world is quite aware of how you look, so you might as well be let in on the secret! Video will very quickly uncover what is not working for you and give you the opportunity to correct it. If you don't have access to a video camera, ask a good friend if he or she notices any repetitive or unusual gestures or expressions you make.

EXERCISES

1. Use vocal variety in your everyday speech. Vary your cadence, your tone, and your volume. Review the vocal warm-up exercises in Chapter 4 in particular. Make the variety logical. Pause before an important point and then increase the volume. Emphasize a keyword by taking it up a note from your normal range.

2. Notice what gestures you typically use as you go through your day. Afterward, go to a mirror and see how they look to others. What would make your gestures more effective? If you are continually gesturing with one hand, how about using both? Incorporate your refined gestures into your daily communications until it begins to feel natural.

3. Videotape yourself giving a presentation as you normally would. Watch it several times without comment until you can view it objectively. Now go through the video more carefully, looking at each of the following areas and rate yourself on a scale of one to five.

   Rating: (5 = Perfection—don't change a thing 1 = Needs immediate work.)

   ★ Movement ____

   ★ Gestures ____

   ★ Eye contact ____

   ★ Smile ____

   ★ Vocal variety ____

   ★ Pace ____

   ★ Volume ____

Pick one area at a time to work on each week, starting with the lower-rated categories.

THE CUES:
LISTENING TO THE BUYER

10

"A lot of what acting is, is paying attention."

~Robert Redford

A buyer for the women's fashion department of a large national retailer remains silent after Laura delivers new pricing information for her fall clothing line. Laura continues with her pitch, assuming the buyer has no problem with this news—after all, Laura rationalizes, it's well-known that everyone in her industry is experiencing increased material costs. The buyer tells her to call back next week when she will make her final decision. When Laura follows up, she discovers that she has lost the sale to a competitor. When she asks for an explanation, the buyer replies that while she liked the line, she thought the price increase was unjustified. Had Laura read the buyer more closely, she would have noticed her suddenly crossed arms, slightly narrowed eyes, and lack of engagement during the remainder of the presentation. Unfortunately, Laura missed all the cues. Now she will have to wait until next season to get another shot at this buyer's business.

There is one primary reason why an actor misses his cue: He is not paying attention. He is off-stage, thinking about his last scene. He is on-stage thinking about his next line or the big monologue in Act II. Whereas missing a scene partner's cue can lead to a confusing performance, missing a cue from a prospect can lead to losing a sale. We breeze through a presentation, unaware that the client is tapping her fingers, glancing at her watch, or has had a sudden change in expression. We talk over clients in our enthusiasm to clarify a point or head off an objection. We disregard the yes that sounded suspiciously like a no. A salesperson, like an actor, must be not only confident about her lines and intentions, but she must also remain aware of whether they are being received and how. Missing a cue will be a thing of the past after you acquire the listening skills used by actors.

Acting techniques for listening to your prospect:

☆ Turn a presentation into a dialogue.

☆ Employ animated listening.

☆ Read verbal and nonverbal buying cues.

☆ Listening with your eyes.

We've heard often enough that listening is an important part of sales. Yet, how many times have we jumped in to finish a prospect's sentence for him because we assume we know what he is going to say? How often do we rush to quell an objection before it is even uttered? Actors have a cardinal rule that sellers should take to heart: *Never upstage your scene partner!*

Upstaging is a form of scene-stealing that diverts the attention from one actor to another. A narcissistic actor who is always stealing the spotlight is not considered a good scene partner and is quickly resented by the rest of the cast. Interrupting, talking over or talking down to your prospect, and ignoring nonverbal cues are considered scene-stealing in sales. Drowning out your prospect may get her attention, but ultimately shuts her down—opening up an opportunity for your competition. There are many ways to listen to our prospects—both verbally and nonverbally—that open up new opportunities and insights that may not have otherwise become apparent.

Waiting for Your Cue

Have you ever walked out of a presentation where there were no real objections, questions, or obvious negative reactions, thinking, "They were totally on-board with me!" only to find out later that you didn't win their business? How could your judgment be so off? Chances are, you have only evaluated *your* performance, forgetting that a presentation or sales pitch is only one half of the conversation. If we are only focused on certain recognizable cues such as a question, an objection, an obvious physical reaction to alert us that our client is not in agreement or is not following us, we are treading on uncertain ground.

In acting's early days, when an actor got a part, instead of the entire script, she would receive only her "sides": pieces of the play that included the actor's lines and only a word or sentence fragment of her scene partner's lines to cue her response. Imagine receiving these sides and trying to make sense of your scene.

Your line: I absolutely agree with you.

Cue: ...surely not.

Your line: That's impossible. Harold can't know about this.

Cue: ...must die.

Your line: There's my bus! See you tomorrow.

After receiving their sides, actors would practice their lines without any idea of the content or meaning behind what they were responding to. When they finally arrived at rehearsal, they would be so focused on listening for their cues that they failed to take in what was actually being said. As you can imagine, this made for some rather disjointed dialogue. Similarly, many sellers get so focused on listening for common buyer cues and reactions that they forget to listen to the full meaning and intent of what is being said. The dangers of selective listening are many. What if your prospect doesn't give you the cue you're expecting? What if you aren't paying attention and miss your cue entirely?

For example, take this standard exchange:

You: This additional coverage is 40 dollars more per month,
but it is well worth it.

Prospect cue: Why do I need it?

You: It will ensure that you are covered for any losses that are
due to injury or theft.

Appropriately handled. Now, suppose we hear this cue and leap to
answer it, but in fact, it means something entirely different?

For example:

You: This additional coverage is 40 dollars more per month,
but it is well worth it.

Prospect cue: Why do I need it if—?

You: (cutting him off) It will ensure that you are covered for
any losses that are due to injury or theft.

Although the cue is nearly the same in both scenarios, if the rest of our
prospect's line was actually: "…if I live in a fully insured building with 24-
hour security," your answer would not have made any sense. Your prospect might restate his question. Then again, he might just decide it's not
worth the effort to get you to listen, and he'll check out for the remainder
of the meeting. What if your prospect didn't ask a question at all? Maybe
you would have addressed his concerns at some point, but maybe not. Bottom line is this: If you are just listening for a verbal cue or glaringly obvious
reaction, you are likely to miss your prospect's cue or intent all together.

TURNING A MONOLOGUE INTO A DIALOGUE

Presentations are an opportunity for us to present our product or service
to a captive audience, but too many of us in sales approach it as one long
monologue instead of the customer dialogue that it should be. How many
places in life do we talk for an uninterrupted 30- or 40-minute stretch without
expecting some response or indication that our listener is following us? Under
most any other circumstances, that person would simply get up and walk away.
Presentations, though necessary, are unnatural for both parties. Many of us
get so focused on *presenting* that we don't pay attention to *observing* the constant flow of nonverbal information that is coming from our recipient.

Good actors approach monologues (long speeches where no one else
is talking) as if they were a dialogue. They rely heavily on their scene partner's non-verbal responses to give them feedback to work off of on a

moment-by-moment basis. Incorporating their scene partner's response creates a dynamic two-way conversation that involves the recipient as much as the speaker. As a salesperson, you should also be working off your client's nonverbal reactions and using that feedback to adjust your presentation on a moment-by-moment basis.

One of film's most famous monologues helped win Peter Finch an Oscar in *Network*. Here is part of his two-minute and 47-second diatribe: "...I want you to get up right now. Get up. Go to your windows, open your windows, and stick your head out, and yell, 'I'm as mad as hell and I'm not going to take this anymore!'" Things have got to change my friends. You've got to get mad. You've got to say, 'I'm as mad as hell and I'm not going to take this anymore!'"[1]

Peter's speech can actually be considered a dialogue with his viewers. It is obvious what he wants. He wants them to get up! But they don't get up right away. So he has to explain further and tell them that they need to get mad. But they're obviously not mad enough. How mad do they need to get? They need to get *mad as hell!* He is not just spouting words into thin air; he is trying to incite action from a passive television audience and working off perceived responses.

LISTENING TO VERBAL CUES

Listening is a critical part of the sales process. In his book *Spin Selling,* Neil Rackham proposed that good sellers were not necessarily the best talkers, but instead they were often the best listeners. He found that the best salespeople had a much higher listen-to-talk ratio. For many sellers, this is a difficult skill to master in their haste to tell their story.

ANIMATED LISTENING

Like animated talking, animated listening is an active state, not the passive exercise of *waiting to speak* that many of us treat it as. It is, as Uta Hagen puts it, "listening with your entire being."[2] Any attempt to illustrate or show that you are listening that is not authentic and internally motivated, such as leaning toward the prospect, putting your hand to your ear, raising your eyebrows, and so on, will come across as false and insincere. If you are truly and fully engaged in listening, you won't have to exaggerate your gestures and expressions. Your attention will read loud and clear.

Think of a great scene from a movie where an actor is listening intently. Perhaps there is no movement on his part and only the slightest change in expression, and yet, do we have any doubt that the actor is hanging on every word that the other character is saying and that his entire being is involved in the process?

An incredible example of animated listening can be seen in the 2006 Best Foreign Language Academy Award–winning movie, *The Lives of Others*: A Stasi officer in 1984 East Berlin is assigned to spy on fellow German citizens by listening to tapes received from wiretaps that have been placed in their apartment. Scene after scene shows award-winning actor Ulrich Mühe at his desk, listening to the personal conversations between a couple to whom, simply by listening, he becomes indelibly bound. To watch him listen is truly a wondrous thing. No matter what is revealed (and much is) his listening is intimate, authentic, and compelling. He is captivated, and therefore captivating to watch.

What to listen for.

Discoveries

It is easy to be so focused on our intentions and goals that we fail to notice, not just cues, but new or different things about our prospects, their companies, or their circumstances. We don't always take in the fullness of what they have to say, often stepping on their lines with "Oh yes, everyone says that at first." We are quick to assume we know where they are headed. Yes, we may think we have heard every objection under the sun, but we still need to treat each one as a new and unique discovery, after all, this is the first time *this* client has said it! Instead of jumping the gun, why not let them express themselves and feel heard? "Oh really! Tell me more about why you feel that way, because most of my clients have felt differently" acknowledges your prospect and gives you an opportunity to learn something you may not have known.

What is said

There's a common saying that goes through many sales organizations: *Buyers are liars*. Though I don't doubt that some are (as are some sellers), and I myself have told a white lie or two to get rid of extremely aggressive salespeople, in general, I think it's too easy to blame the buyer. More often than not, people tell us much of what we need to know about them up front, but we choose to hear what we want. It may be conscious or unconscious, but when we consider that everything that is said to us goes through our emotional filter and is colored by our expectations, hopes, fears, wishes, and past experiences, it's a wonder that we can hear each other at all!

I once took on a prospective home buyer as a client after she had informed me that she had not been satisfied with her former broker after a year of looking for a home. She explained that she had one house under contract, but backed out after finding some issues during the inspection. Although the inspection situation was a red flag, I didn't press her on it. After taking her to see only a few homes, I was pleasantly surprised when she decided to write a contract on one. Right after it went under contract, the script started to unfold: She didn't like the HOA requirements, the building was too close to a fire station, the market was unstable. I listened to her and carefully tried to address her concerns. However, the day before the inspection, she backed out of the contract for a seemingly insignificant reason. Why was I surprised?

I realized at once that I had taken the facts of her situation and interpreted them through my own personal filter and it came out something like this: *She didn't have success before because she wasn't working with me.* I don't like to admit that my ego got in the way of selling, but how many of us have disregarded pertinent facts by telling ourselves, "It's going to be different for me"? Though there's no denying that people can occasionally surprise you, in my experience, people tell you who they are in a variety of different ways and it's up to us to listen.

I learned from this experience (and unfortunately a few others) that if you really want to know where a prospect stands, you need to turn off your filter when he speaks: Don't anticipate, project, or make excuses for your prospect. Don't tune out the negative because you really need the sale. Listen to not only *what* he says, but *how* he says it. Every word, gesture, or pause provides you with new information. For example, try saying yes in the following ways: warmly, impatiently, politely, patronizingly. One word can have many different meanings, so if you're not getting the response you are looking for, ask yourself what steps you need to take to get things back on track. Do you need to go over a point in greater detail? Provide an example? Ask him to explain? If his answer seems incongruent or inappropriate, don't just let it go. Remember: Maybe he's not lying—maybe you're just not listening.

What is not said

Often what a prospect doesn't say is as important as what he does say. If you have just made an important point or announcement that typically causes a reaction and you don't get one, stop. That is noteworthy. Give him a chance to show that he has received it. If you are expecting a response and are greeted by silence, ask if you have fully explained it, how he feels about it, or what his thoughts are. Don't mistake silence for agreement, or, like Laura, you may be waiting another year for a sale.

Listening With Your Eyes

Question: After you've made an important point, you look at your client. Her arms are tightly crossed, and she has a skeptical expression on her face. You ask if she is in agreement. She says yes. What do you do?

A. Continue on with the rest of your presentation.

B. Ask if she has any questions or concerns with what you've just said. If she says no, continue on with your presentation.

C. Ask if she has any questions or concerns with what you've just said and if she says no, add: "The reason I ask is that some clients initially have concerns about this, but have found that because of (provide evidence to support your point) it becomes irrelevant."

C is by far the best answer when you consider that 55 percent of communication is visual. If we ignore body language and facial expressions, we may be losing more than half of our prospect's message! Often we can learn more about what a prospect is thinking or feeling through nonverbal communication than we can by listening to an entire speech. It's critical to be aware of nonverbal communication not only when the prospect is speaking, but when he's not speaking as well. Ms. Hagen calls it "listening with your eyes."[3] Nonverbal communication includes facial expression, gestures, body language, and use of space. Look for the actions and reactions while you're speaking, and how they change before and during their response. If your prospect's words are incongruent with her body language or facial expression, as in the previous example, stop and clarify what that means.

Some of us are better at reading body language than others. The following is an excellent acting exercise for learning to quickly read the body language of others and respond to the slightest changes. Unlike most of the exercises in this book, this one does require two people.

The Repetition Exercise.

Repetition is one of the most fundamental acting exercises taught in acting academies across the country. Developed by Sanford Meisner, it involves two actors facing each other and "repeating" their observations about one another back and forth.[4] For example, the first actor might note that the other actor is smiling and say: "You're smiling." The second actor repeats back: "I'm smiling." This goes back and forth until one of the actors notices a change in mood, expression, or behavior of the other actor. Then he might say: "You're frowning," and the second actor repeats: "I'm frowning." In this way, actors learn to spontaneously observe and respond to changes in their scene partner, listen, and react truthfully. I've seen actors go from self-conscious staring, to gut-splitting laughter, to full-on tears. Something powerful happens when we really look and listen to each other.

Reading Cues

The study of body language is known as kinesics.[5] Though the following general rules won't make you an expert on body language, they may help you read some of your prospects' attitudes and feelings more accurately than by just listening to their words:

☆ Consider gestures and expressions as a whole, not just individually. For example, if the arms are crossed, but the smile is warm and authentic, the eyes are focused and smiling, perhaps the arms are only an indication that the person is cold.

☆ Listen to your gut. We all have an innate ability to read other people's body language, so your intuition may be picking up something that you may consciously have missed. Don't ignore it.

☆ Don't be misled by unique body language. Some people have certain gestures or expressions that they make that have nothing to do with what is being said, such as blinking quickly, stroking their hair, or rubbing their hands together. Be sure to distinguish this from other unusual gestures before you make assumptions.

☆ Look for displacement gestures. Often when people are feeling ambiguous, they look to release energy and emotions through their bodies by tapping their feet, drumming their fingers, or crossing and recrossing their legs. If you've just brought up a price increase and your client starts rhythmically touching her finger to the side of her face, you'd better do some explaining!

☆ Note any unusual eye contact. If a person is watching you intently, it can mean that she is with you, or it can mean she doesn't want to take her eyes off of you because she doesn't trust you. Lack of eye contact can mean loss of interest or disbelief, but it can also simply mean that the other person is uncomfortable making direct eye contact. If she's looking at you, but her eyes seem slightly unfocused, it's likely that she is bored and you need to do something to shake things up immediately.

☆ Look for incongruent behavior and words. If the words don't match your prospect's body language or expression, do some further observing.

☆ Look for sudden changes in body language or expression. Do they correlate with something controversial you've brought up? Are they related to any particular subject?

☆ Weed out the lies. Touching the face, excessive blinking, or not blinking at all can indicate that a person is lying.

☆ Keep in mind that cultural differences greatly affect the meaning of body language. In Middle Eastern cultures, extended periods of eye contact are common, whereas Americans prefer more intermittent eye contact and many Asian cultures consider prolonged eye contact rude or disrespectful.[6]

Reading body language is not an exact science, and there are exceptions to every rule. However, if we are armed with a basic understanding, and our gut and our eyes, we will have a better-than-average chance of grasping our prospect's true needs and feelings, and evaluating whether our message is being properly received. Your ability to read and understand a prospect's nonverbal responses is another tool that can give you a huge edge on your competition.

EXERCISES

1. Watch a really great movie monologue, such as: Clint Eastwood in *Dirty Harry,* Robin Williams in *Good Will Hunting,* Hillary Swank in *Million Dollar Baby,* or Jack Nicholson in *A Few Good Men.* Look for moments where they connect and respond to their scene partner's nonverbal reactions.

2. Grab a friend or co-worker and try the repetition exercise. Make sure you change your comments only to reflect something new: a new expression, behavior, or gesture. Stick with it for at least five minutes, even when it gets uncomfortable. You will be surprised to find how much you learn from this exercise—not just about others, but about yourself.

3. Practice animated listening with your clients and prospects for one day. See how many new things you can discover about your existing clients and how much you can learn about a new prospect by focusing on both verbal and nonverbal responses.

THE PROPS:
STAGING A SALE

11

"When I used to do musical theatre, my dad refused to come backstage. He never wanted to see the props up close or the sets up close. He didn't want to see the magic."

~Nia Vardalos

Karen is the leasing agent for a new luxury high-rise off Chicago's popular Michigan Avenue. Most of her business comes from walk-ins, and when potential buyers view a video presentation that highlights the building's many unique features and amenities, Karen has an impressive conversion rate. But when one promising couple sits down to watch her presentation, the screen freezes and Karen is lost. After several minutes spent trying to determine the problem, she reboots the computer and another five minutes passes; when this doesn't work, she calls in an AV expert. After 15 minutes of waiting for help to arrive and fix the problem, Karen finally gets the presentation back on track. Unfortunately, by this time, the couple has talked themselves out of the building, deciding instead to look for something less pricey. Her walk-in business has walked out the door. Karen lost their attention—and a potential big sale.

When an actor breaks or drops something on stage and steps out of character to apologize to the audience or comment on it, he has "broken character." Not only does the actor lose his focus, but he also pulls the audience out of the magic of the play and the belief in his character. Just like in *The Wizard of Oz*, once Toto pulls the curtain away, revealing that the Great and Powerful Oz is merely a second-rate magician from Omaha, there is no going back to the Emerald City. It is difficult—if not impossible—when an actor breaks that bond of trust with the audience for them to regain it.

Props can enhance an actor's performance or detract from it. The same holds true for salespeople. A powerful video or PowerPoint presentation can add depth and dazzle to your presentation, but a faulty demo or shoddy handout can diminish your credibility. If you've put in the necessary work to build a compelling and persuasive presentation, don't let a bad prop tear it all down. Learn how to use props properly and save the show when the audience gets a glimpse of the wizard behind the curtain!

Acting techniques for using sales props:

☆ How and when to effectively use sales props.

☆ How to avoid prop malfunctions.

☆ How to keep the show going.

Sales Props

In the theater, a prop is any object held or used on stage by an actor to further the plot or the action of the play. In the same way, sales props refer to anything used by a salesperson to further the action of the sale.

Common sales props:

☆ PowerPoint.

☆ White boards.

☆ Flip charts.

☆ Videos.

☆ Product model or sample.

☆ Handouts.

Whatever you choose to use to support your presentation, the purpose should be the same as a theatrical prop, to further the action. Keeping this goal in mind will help you determine what is and isn't useful to include in your client meeting or presentation. You may have an exciting new video showing your company president on a recent fundraising trip to India. However, if your goal is to show a furniture dealer how you can move some of his inventory, you may want to reconsider your choice.

Selecting a prop is an important decision. Although many of us rely on whatever prop our company provides for us, the same prop may not be suitable for every client or situation. A white board may make sense for a large group, but be too formal for a one-on-one meeting. Too many different props may confuse your audience and dilute your message. Here are some considerations to keep in mind when selecting props for your presentation:

☆ **How does it read?** Theater directors insist that a prop reads well from the audience. They test it to make sure it can be seen from the last row of the theater. You, too, want to ensure that your prop "reads well" from your audience. Whereas demonstrating a small handheld device may work well for a group of two or three, a room full of busy executives may grow impatient straining to see it. A flip chart might work just fine for a small group, but get lost in a large boardroom.

☆ **Who is your audience?** Are they sophisticated executives used to viewing high-tech, multimedia presentations? Or are they seat-of-the-pants buyers who want something they can physically touch and hold? When I was selling radio advertising, I would often find myself competing against television and print, which some buyers preferred because they could experience it both visually, and, in the case of print, tactilely as well. I discovered that by providing a printed copy of a sample commercial or showing a video of a station event, I could get on more equal footing with this type of prospect.

☆ **What is the purpose?** Are you adding visual cues to help your prospects follow along or to clarify a point? Are you demonstrating a new feature or unique benefit? Are you comparing your product to a competitor's? The purpose should always be to help communicate the message, but different sub-purposes can help determine the best prop to use. Although some props are entertaining or visually stunning, if they don't support the message, ask yourself if they are necessary. The chandelier flying across the theater in *The Phantom of the Opera* was thrilling, but does anyone remember what was taking place in the scene?

Why use props?

Props can enhance your presentation and support your message in a variety of ways by:

☆ Increasing listener retention.

☆ Emphasizing key points.

☆ Demonstrating product or service.

☆ Simplifying and clarifying information.

☆ Breaking up monotony.

☆ Providing seller cues.

Let's look at each of these points in greater detail and determine how you can best use them in your presentation or pitch.

Increasing listener retention

According to Toastmasters International, on average, listeners only retain 10 percent of what they've heard one week later. This percentage increases to 67 when visual aids are added to the equation.[1] If you want a prospect to remember what you've said, visual components can be extremely valuable in increasing their retention.

Emphasizing key points

Props should be used to underscore key points. If you have your entire presentation on PowerPoint for your prospect to follow along as you read from each slide, you not only give her little reason to listen to you, but you dilute the message. By trying to make everything important, you often make nothing stand out. Try to limit your major points to one per slide.

Demonstrating product or service

Often there is no greater sales tool than the product or service itself. If your product lends itself to being demonstrated or sampled by the prospect, you are adding not just a visual component, but a tactile one as well.

I experienced a powerful firsthand example of this after winning a drawing at a networking event I recently attended. The prize was a set of bath products from Arbonne International, a natural beauty product line only available through direct sellers. When the company representative contacted me and asked if she could drop it off in person when she was in the neighborhood, I felt I owed her the courtesy of meeting her, even though I knew I would not be purchasing anything from her. I listened politely to some of the features that make Arbonne's products unique and found much of what she had to say intriguing—or hypothetically intriguing, if I was interested, which I wasn't. She casually gave me a product brochure, pointed out a few items that she loved, and mentioned that the best way to really understand how their products were different was to use the entire line for a few days. I started to explain that I really wasn't interested in trying a new skincare line when she pulled out six full-size products in their distinctive orange packaging and said she would be happy to leave them with me for a few days. I hesitated, knowing I risked getting her hopes up if I accepted this offer, but the appeal was too great. Could these products really make the difference in which she seemed to so fervently believe? So I agreed, but telling myself that I would *not* be "guilted" into buying them just because she offered to let me try them.

During the next few days, I used the products religiously and found myself wondering, *was it my imagination or was my face really glowing and the lines receding*? When she called three days later to arrange to pick them up, I felt a pang; they had become part of my daily routine, they seemed to be working—and they looked so nice on my bathroom counter! When she arrived, I was an easy sale. I am confident that a large part of Arbonne's 100 percent annual growth in much of the last decade is due to allowing customers to not only try the product, but to take ownership.[2]

Were the props relevant to the message? Yes, absolutely. Did the props further the action? You bet. Your product might not lend itself to sampling (a million-dollar medical device, for example), but there are still many other creative ways to use props to reinforce your message and make sure it is remembered.

Simplifying and clarifying information

Some products and services are complex, multi-part offerings. Even if your prospect is familiar with how they work, he or she can get lost in the sheer volume of facts and statistics. Don't make your prospect work too hard to follow along or only the most dogged will stay with you. Stick to the rule of threes: If you introduce a topic that has three or more parts to it, provide a visual reference so the prospect knows where you are. This also helps frame things. For example, if I were doing this section as a PowerPoint presentation, I would have all six points on the slide and let the listeners know that we are now on number four. If you use more than three figures or statistics, make those visual as well.

Breaking up monotony

As discussed in the previous chapter, no matter how compelling your subject, your listener's attention will start to wane during the length of the average presentation. Adult learners can keep tuned in to a lecture for no more than 15 to 20 minutes at a time.[3] By using a new prop at key times within your presentation, you can re-engage them by giving them something new to focus on.

Providing seller cues

When we go to the theater, we expect the actor to be "off-book"— in other words, not stumbling through his script or constantly calling out "Line, please!" Why should prospects expect any less from us? Many businesspeople—not just sellers—use PowerPoint as a crutch, rather than the prospect retention tool that it was designed to be. We're afraid we're not going to remember what the next point is. We're not quite sure of the statistics. Though it's acceptable to use your presentation to provide cues, relying on it too heavily is simply lazy. It makes for an ineffective presentation and encourages reading the slide to the listener, the kiss of death in PowerPoint presentations. If you can't get through your presentation without looking at each screen, go back to Chapter 6 and work on the steps for rehearsing a business script. You should not be learning the information at the same time as your prospect. You are the expert. Be prepared.

How to Use Props Dramatically

Used correctly, props afford us the opportunity to create memorable moments or experiences. When possible, look for the following opportunities to add drama to your presentation:

☆ **The dramatic pause.** A well-planned moment of silence before unveiling a prop can build anticipation and add drama, just as pausing before an important point when we speak.

☆ **The dramatic presentation.** When to reveal your prop is an important decision. Leaving a demo out on the prospect's desk until its proper time invites questions before you may be ready to address them. Digging it out of the bottom of your briefcase is distracting and probably not the image you'd like to portray. Keeping a prop veiled and off to the side until ready to present it at just the right moment adds an element of intrigue and anticipation.

☆ **The dramatic display.** The way we handle a prop informs the audience how they should view it. A glass-encrusted plastic crown can take on the significance of a treasure beyond imagination if it's treated with the proper reverence by the actor. Even if your demo has traveled from Boise to Boston, or you have a hundred more samples in the trunk of your car, if you treat it with awe and respect, your prospect will endow it with greater value as well.

PROP MALFUNCTIONS

The thing about props is that at some point, they are very likely to malfunction or disappear. The following definition of a prop from *The Community Theater Dictionary* sums it up: "Prop: A hand-carried object small enough to be lost by an actor 30 seconds before it is needed on stage."[4]

Mistakes in the theater are legendary: slips and falls on stage, guns that fail to go off, scenery that moves unexpectedly, and even the rare death when a prop sword was replaced by the real thing in a 1672 production of the ill-fated *Macbeth* in Amsterdam.[5] More recently, four actors were hurt before the most expensive production in Broadway history, *Spider-Man: Turn Off the Dark*, even opened its doors.[6] Though most mistakes are less dramatic, they can still negatively affect the actors' performances and the audience's overall experience.

I was in a Neil Simon show that, during the course of an eight-week run, had at least five prop malfunctions, all involving me. The doorknob came off in my hand, the phone didn't ring at the right time, there was no liquid in a bottle from which I was supposed to pour a drink, and the purse that was supposed to contain cash to tip the doorman was stuffed with underwear from an earlier scene strike. Although none of these was a "showstopper" or required breaking character, in the case of the doorknob, I'm not sure the audience ever bought into the rest of the show. Most of these mistakes could have been avoided had I checked my props prior to each night's performance. But I got lazy, relying on others to handle my preparation, or expecting things to be just as I left them.

Mistakes can either temporarily or permanently stop the forward motion of the play and take the audience out of the magic an actor has worked so hard to create. They can also stop the forward motion of your sale. They can be as serious as when Will Smith's character in *The Pursuit of Happyness* has everything invested in selling medical equipment and it fails to perform during a demonstration. Or they can be as common as your PowerPoint presentation freezing during a presentation, your demo breaking, or your samples being left behind. Regardless, it is the way in which you handle these mishaps that will determine whether your meeting moves forward or comes to a screeching halt.

Acting Tips for Working With Prop Failures

✩ **Use it.** If an actor makes a mistake, but uses it in the scene, the audience usually goes along with it, without being any wiser. If it doesn't affect the basic intention or message of your presentation, there's no need to draw attention to it. If it's a mistake that you can incorporate into your presentation, all the better. Spontaneity sometimes spices things up and can add for some interesting impromptu moments.

✩ **Lose it.** If the AV equipment breaks down or the flash drive isn't communicating with the computer port, know when to let it go and work your backup plan (see page 158). Five minutes is about as long as you can expect an audience to remain still and patient while you search for a solution. After that, you need to lose the prop and carry on with the show. Keep your cool and don't be too upset about it (even if it is film-festival quality). If it was noticeable, apologize once and then move on. If you keep apologizing or repeating, "if I had my demo with me you'd be able to see this…" your prospect will start to wonder what she's missing and lose focus. If your prop is so important that you can't go on without it, I suggest you rethink your presentation.

✩ **Laugh at it.** During the Broadway run of *Wicked*, Kristin Chenoweth as Glinda the Good Witch hit her wand on the bed and accidentally broke it. She immediately threw it offstage and ad-libbed: "It's a training wand anyway," then moved on as the audience laughed.[7]

Laughing at your mistakes is an important skill to master. People typically respond positively to someone who can make a mistake and keep going on with good humor. You can even carry the joke into the rest of the presentation. You'll learn more on how to work with mistakes through improv in Chapter 13.

How to Avoid Mistakes

Actors can be quite superstitious and offer a history of colorful tricks and techniques for preventing problems on stage, including: avoid real food, fresh flowers, jewelry, or Bibles on stage; cats are good luck, unless they walk across the stage (which makes you wonder how the musical *Cats* enjoyed such a successful run!); do not whistle backstage or on-stage; do not mention the play *Macbeth.* Instead, refer to it as "the Scottish play" or be prepared to leave the theater, spin around three times, spit, curse, and then knock to be allowed back in; do not accept offerings of "good luck." Instead ask well-wishers to say "break a leg," to avoid tempting fate to knock you down for your good fortune.[8]

Although any or all of these may be effective (who knows?) there are more practical ways for avoiding potential prop pitfalls in both sales and the theater:

☆ **Check your props.** Take a lesson from the theater and always check your props before a presentation, even if you've done it a hundred times, even if your assistant has assured you that everything is ready. Things are not always where you left them, or in the condition you left them, and it will be during that one big meeting when the president of the company pops in that your key prop disappears. Remember: No one cares more about your presentation than you do.

☆ **Rehearse with your props.** Adding a prop requires adjustments in your presentation. If you're using a PowerPoint, you need to make sure you are not standing in front of it or talking to it. If you're using a white board, you need to ensure that your writing is large and legible, and that you don't speak with your back to your audience. If you have a demo or a video, you want to make sure you have proper lighting and it's visible to everyone in your audience. If you have handouts, predetermine when you will distribute them and avoid verbally delivering any important information at that time, as your audience's attention will be on the handouts, and not you.

✩ **Have a backup plan.** Smart salespeople always have their presentation in several different places: on their computer, a flash drive, the Web, and in hard copy. If time allows, they ship proposals, samples, or demos to their destination ahead of time. Don't be caught empty-handed unless you are anxious to try out your improv skills.

✩ **Know your presentation.** Most of this book is geared toward perfecting your number-one selling tool: yourself. Don't rely too heavily on technology to carry your message, or you will easily be beat out by the guy with the even newer technology. In the old days, sellers didn't have PowerPoint, videos, or even color copies. Can you imagine? It was up to them to sell their product or service. Make sure you are still capable of doing the same by practicing your presentation without the props. You will quickly be able to determine whether you are using a prop to "prop up" your presentation.

Great presentation skills and an engaging, on-message, audience-appropriate prop is a winning combination for any presentation.

EXERCISES

1. Determine what primary purpose a prop will play in your presentation and which prop best serves that purpose, as well as your audience.

2. Decide at which point within your presentation you can add a dramatic pause, dramatic presentation, or display.

3. Rehearse your presentation with your prop in front of a co-worker or the mirror to make sure your prop is visible at all times and that you are not talking to it.

4. Rehearse your presentation as you would give it if you did not have your prop.

5. Come up with two backup plans in case your prop fails or disappears.

THE AUDIENCE: OVERCOMING FEAR

12

"If you give an audience a chance they will do half your acting for you."

~Katharine Hepburn

Lisa is naturally enthusiastic and at ease when meeting with individual clients about how she can help them with their Website design, but freezes up when she has to present to a group. She becomes painfully aware of all eyes in the room upon her, her mouth goes dry, her heart races, and her knees feel as if they might give out. As Lisa begins to speak, she grows increasingly self-conscious about that tremble in her voice and draws a blank at a key point within her presentation. Frustrated with her performance, Lisa is not surprised when she is unable to close the deal. Before her next group presentation, Lisa is coached to focus on a specific object in the room until she feels grounded, gradually expanding her circle of attention as she grows more comfortable. This time, Lisa's personality and persuasive powers are not upstaged by her anxiety and she easily wins the client's business.

Naturally gregarious and knowledgeable about the custom sports products that he sells to local sporting goods stores, Joel gets nervous and tongue-tied when he gets the opportunity to pitch to executives at a major sports team. He rushes through his presentation, skimming over important points, and hesitating when it comes time to ask for the business. When Joel gets a second chance, he works on using his imagination to transform his executive prospect into one of his friendly, easy-going sporting goods clients. His salesmanship shines, and he moves seamlessly through to the close.

If you're not always comfortable in the spotlight, you're not alone. Public speaking continues to hold the top spot in the list of fears of the general population. And not all great salespeople are fearless extroverts, either. According to a recent study of 199,000 employed salespeople across a variety of companies, industries, and countries, almost 20 percent said they were uncomfortable starting conversations with someone. In one study in the UK, more than 30 percent of the salespeople surveyed said they were reluctant to engage others in conversation![1] When your livelihood is dependent upon engaging others in conversation, that creates a lot of inner tension.

Actors are no strangers to stage fright. Laurence Olivier reportedly had to be pushed on stage by his stage manager during one London run. Later in her career, Barbra Streisand developed such debilitating stage fright after forgetting the words to a song at a Central Park concert that she couldn't sing in public for almost three decades.[2] Although these are extreme examples, many actors experience stage fright of lesser magnitude and learn how to manage it—or even use it to enhance their performance—through a variety of tools that are as effective on Broadway as they are in the boardroom.

Actors' secrets for coping with stage fright:

☆ Channeling pre-performance energy into a positive force.

☆ Using circles of attention.

☆ Creating privacy in front of groups.

☆ The Marsha Brady technique.

WHAT IS STAGE FRIGHT?

Whether you are making a presentation to a crowd of 300 or an intimate group of three, the symptoms of stage fright, or performance anxiety, vary from person to person, but may include some or all of the following: shortness of breath, dry mouth, racing heart, shaky voice, blushing, sweating, trembling, and even nausea. Anxiety triggers our sympathetic nervous system, dumping adrenaline into our blood stream, and it signals our bodies' "fight or flight" reaction.[3] Wheras this is an important physiological reaction when confronted with danger, it can be disasterous when giving a presentation. Stage fright can happen to actors, speakers, performers, and businesspeople; anyone who has to perform in front of others is a potential victim. Stage fright can be broken down into several different causess. See if you recognize any of these culprits.

Fear of Being Judged

Often, an actor can perform at ease in front of a crowded house, but put one critic in the front row, and he experiences severe stage fright. Like Joel in the previous example, who froze up in front of VIPs, the fear of being negatively judged—especially by someone we perceive as important— is a leading cause of stage fright.

Early in my acting career, I much preferred an anonymous audience to a familiar one. I often neglected to tell friends and family that I was even *in* a show, prompting one boyfriend to refer to me as a "secret actress." By using the tools outlined in this chapter, I was able to successfully overcome that fear and now enjoy having friends and family in the audience.

Fear of Negative Expectations

Expecting negative outcomes can create a self-fulfilling prophecy; an actor worries about forgetting a line and, sure enough, he does. We worry about forgetting our presentation, and that's just what we do. We imagine that the prospect isn't going to be interested, and we end up giving a lackluster presentation.

Fear of Hyper Self-consciousness

When an actor is painfully aware of being observed by an audience, he often starts observing himself. This self-examination takes the actor away from his performance and out of the moment. I'm sure we've all experienced that detached "out-of-body" sensation of watching ourselves doing something frightening. Like Lisa in our example, the slightest flaw (her trembling voice) takes on monumental proportions, and we become more involved in our self-analysis than delivering our message.

Fear About our Ability to Perform

When we lack confidence in our knowledge of the material, or our ability to present it, stage fright has a much greater chance of taking hold. Most actors have that nightmare of being on stage and not knowing their lines—even though they may have spent weeks and months rehearsing them. It is not uncommon to forget a line or two on stage, just as it is not uncommon to forget parts of your presentation. Once it happens, the actual event is rarely as devastating as we imagine. In fact, we often relax as we realize that we can rebound from mistakes without losing a client or a sale. As Jack Nicholson said: "Once you've been really bad in a movie, there's a certain kind of fearlessness you develop."

Tips for Preventing Stage Fright

Before we look at techniques for handling performance anxiety once it hits, here are some tips for how to prevent—or at least lessen—the odds of stage fright taking hold of you in the first place.

☆ **Be prepared.** Know your material inside and out. (There it is again!) This basic step can go a long way toward preventing stage fright. If you follow the steps in Chapter 6, you will fully understand what you are saying and why, and you will have properly rehearsed it. This will give you confidence in your material. If you follow the physical warm-ups in Chapter 4, you will be loose and relaxed and know how to say it. This will give you confidence in your ability to present it.

☆ **Have a destination.** When I walk out on stage, I always know what my first destination is and why, and it gives me the confidence I need to start the scene. If your body does not have a reason to move and a place to move to, you are likely to feel awkward and self-conscious, which, unchecked, can lead to performance anxiety. As discussed in Chapter 9, it's helpful to have some set destination points to go to during your presentation. If your body feels purposeful, your mind will as well.

☆ **Focus on an activity.** Doing a demonstration, presenting a slide show, and writing on a white board all offer us opportunities to direct our focus *on* a presentation-related activity and *off* of our performance. The more involved the activity, the busier our minds are and the less time we have to take our emotional temperature.

☆ **Stay in the moment.** Most fear is located in the future or the past, not the present. *What if I forget a key point? I shouldn't have just said that!* If you stay in the moment and focus on everything that is happening "right now," as opposed to projecting a future outcome or regretting a previous action, you can keep the negative thinking from spiraling out of control.

It's often frightening when actors finally go "off-book," or run the scene without relying on their script. But once they let go of the lines and trust that their words will come out as a natural response to their scene partner, they are more engaged in the scene and the fear leaves them. The same holds true for salespeople. If you have internalized your presentation, you can focus on working off of your prospect from moment-to-moment, leaving less room for fear to creep in.

☆ **Use a strong "Moment Before."** The good news about stage fright is that it is hard to maintain an intense level of anxiety for an extended period of time. Often a powerful and positive "Moment Before" can carry you through the first few minutes of a presentation—which is typically when anxiety is at its worst. Actors generally suffer the most while waiting backstage to go on and during the first few minutes of their performance. If they get through that (and most do) their rehearsal preparation kicks in and they are able to ease into their role. In the same way, if you use a strong "Moment Before" to get through the first few minutes of your presentation, you will likely be able to relax into your role.

☆ **Move your body.** If you watched me prepare backstage before a show, you might think I was warming up for a race. I pace, stretch, shake my legs and arms, throw punches, and take a lot of deep breaths and long exhales. Moving the body, especially the large muscle groups, is one of the best things you can do to relieve pre-performance anxiety. It focuses all of that pent-up anxiety and energy pulsing through your body, gives it a much-needed release, and redirects it into the scene or presentation. Instead of feeling like jumping out of your skin before your next presentation, moving your body will make you feel energized and ready to go, free to focus on your presentation and your audience.

Acting Techniques for Managing Stage Fright.

You've tried all of the previous suggestions, but still feel butterflies in front of a group. Don't worry, even the pros need help sometimes. Try the following acting techniques proven to successfully reduce stage fright to manageable levels.

1. Channeling pre-performance anxiety into positive energy

Rather than dreading it, actors often rely on pre-performance anxiety to kick-start them into a dynamic performance. The poster boy for anxious characters, the late, great Jack Lemmon put it this way: "Without heightened apprehension, an actor probably won't give as good a performance as he should."[4]

Attempting to eliminate your anxiety entirely can go so far as to drain all of the enthusiasm and energy out of your performance. Uta Hagen tells the story of "talking herself out of nerves" before the opening of a Broadway show at the young age of 22. To alleviate her pre-performance anxiety, she told herself that the whole event, the audience, the critics, the performance, didn't matter and that she didn't care. Ms. Hagen's disappointing performance convinced her of her mistake.[5]

Instead of getting rid of stage fright, try channeling it into positive energy that will work to enhance your performance. A simple way to do this is to *re-label anxiety as excitement.* Excitement and anxiety are closely related. They often produce similar symptoms and both result in an increase in tension or energy. When you're anxious, your tendency is to become more inhibited. When you're excited, you become less inhibited.[6] By re-labeling those nervous feelings as excitement and pleasant anticipation rather than fear and dread, you can turn this energy outward and become more engaged in your presentation and your audience, which will make you feel increasingly confident.

2. Using circles of attention

Actors can get overwhelmed and intimidated by the stage, the lights, and the audience; they can become self-conscious and lose their bearing once on stage if they are not focused. Stanislavski developed an exercise to address this common problem: An actor concentrates his attention on a small circle around him, which includes one other actor or a prop.After he feels firmly grounded in this small circle, he starts to expand his focus to a larger circle, including perhaps another actor or prop, and continues to enlarge his focus. In this way, he relaxes into each circle. If he loses his concentration at any point, the actor simply goes back to placing his focus on the small circle and starts the process over again.[7]

You can easily apply this same technique to sales. When in a group of any size, focus your attention on one person until you start to feel comfortable, then widen your circle to include another, and another, until you are eventually taking in the whole room with ease. The key is to really concentrate on that first person, using all of the communication skills you've learned in previous chapters.

If your focus is powerful enough, it will be nearly impossible for you to worry about what others are thinking of you at the same time. One caveat: When you do this, try not to obviously exclude others by turning your back to them or talking too quietly for them to hear. Simply focus in on one person and within a short amount of time you will be comfortable taking in the entire room.

3. Creating privacy

In an increasingly noisy and crowded world, most of us have become experts at creating privacy in some pretty un-private places, such as in the middle of a coffee shop, dining at a crowded restaurant, riding on the bus, and so on. I was at a cafe in New York where the tables were so close— literally less than 6 inches apart—I could have reached over and wiped the crumbs off one gentleman's beard. And yet, I was able to have a private conversation with my dining partner, and the diners on both sides of me seemed to be able to do the same. I might be able to tell you a few things they were talking about, but for the most part, I was involved in my own conversation. How is it that we are able to do that? By focusing so intently on the person to whom we are speaking, we often block others out of our awareness. The greater our focus on the other person, the less our ability to think about our fears, or what others around us are thinking.

4. The Marsha Brady technique

I coined this after the famous "Driver's Seat" episode from *The Brady Bunch* to describe a specific use of the acting technique, substitution, which we discussed in Chapter 8. In this episode, Marsha is attempting to get her driver's license, but she becomes so overcome with anxiety that she chokes before she even pulls away from the curb, failing the test. Before she retakes the test, Mike Brady suggests that she visualize the instructor in his underwear to overcome her fear. When she starts to panic, she takes his advice, the fear passes, and she passes the test with flying colors.

You don't have to picture your prospect in his underwear, but like Joel at the beginning of this chapter, you can use substitution to imagine that you are speaking to a less intimidating audience to relieve some of your fear and anxiety. Review the steps for substitution in Chapter 8.

A SALES PRO SCENE: "MANAGING PRESENTATION ANXIETY"

THE CAST

SHARON: A financial consultant.

RANDALL: A seemingly critical prospect.

THE SETTING

In order to generate new business, it is common in the financial planning industry to host informational seminars on topical subjects such as how to repair poor credit or consolidate debt. Although Sharon has helped dozens of clients realize their financial goals, she was tongue-tied and unfocused at her first seminar and failed to convert any prospects into clients.

DIRECTOR'S SCENE NOTES:

JH

Describe what you were feeling before your seminar.

SHARON

I felt shaky and jumpy; I was worried I was going to forget what I wanted to say, or not sound professional or knowledgeable. Randall, an older gentleman seated in the front row, was staring at me with his arms crossed and a skeptical expression on his face all night. Every time I looked at him, I lost track and confidence.

JH

How do you normally feel when you're talking to a client one on one about their financial options?

SHARON

I feel confident and helpful, as if I have something valuable to offer.

                              JH

It must be difficult for people to talk to strangers about
their financial situation. How do you put prospective cli-
                         ents at ease?

                            SHARON

I explain to them that it's very common to experience
credit problems and debt, and that they are not alone. In
fact, they are ahead of most people because they are taking
the first step to deal with it. I let them know that there
is a solution and it's not as frightening as they imagine
                      it's going to be.

                              JH

That is exactly what I am going to tell you: It is very
common to experience the feelings you did before your presentation, but there is a solution. And, you are ahead of
most people because you are taking steps to handle it!

                            SHARON
                            Great.

                              JH

Do you remember what your expectations were before the
                          seminar?

                            SHARON

I assumed I'd be a little uncomfortable because I don't
like speaking in front of groups and I thought I might
forget a few things, but honestly, I didn't expect to feel
                    as anxious as I did.

                              JH
                   Who was judging you?

                            SHARON
            The audience. Especially Randall.

                              JH
                     Are you sure?

                            SHARON
                   What do you mean?

JH

Did Randall and the others really come out on a cold week-night in November to grade your performance? Or perhaps, were they really concerned about their financial status and hoping to get some help?

SHARON

I see what you mean.

JH

I think the only judge may have been you. And judging your-self actually got in the way of giving valuable advice to these people. Not to change the subject, but I understand you were recently married. How did you feel just before you walked down the aisle?

SHARON

Oh God. I was a bundle of nerves, shaky, breathless. I wasn't sure I was going to be able to get the words out when it was time to exchange vows!

JH

So how did you get through it?

SHARON

I knew I was just really excited and that there wasn't any-thing to fear. It was all in my head. I reminded myself that everyone there loved me and wanted the best for me. And once I saw my husband standing at the end of the aisle, all of my focus went to him. I don't think I even noticed the audi-ence after that, and the rest of the ceremony just flew by.

JH

So those symptoms you described as excitement—shaky, breathless, forgetful—aren't those similar to the words you used to describe your anxiety before your presentation?

SHARON

Yes. I guess they are.

JH

Is it possible you were excited about your presentation?

SHARON

Hmm. I hadn't thought of it that way, but it is exciting to think you can help change someone's life for the better, help them get out of debt, buy a home, send a child to college. And getting a new client is always exciting.

JH

So if you were to re-label those pre-presentation feelings as excitement, as opposed to anxiety, do you think that would help you?

SHARON

That might work. I'll sure try it!

JH

One last thing. When you were walking down the aisle, you managed to block out the fact that a hundred pairs of eyeballs were focused on you and move through your fear. How did you do that?

SHARON

I just concentrated on my husband who was smiling back at me, and it calmed me right down. I thought about our new life together and I couldn't wait to get up there and say "I do."

JH

You've proven that you have the ability to focus, so try using it the next time you give a seminar. Start by focusing your attention on one person and thinking about helping that individual improve his or her financial situation. Once you start to feel more confident try expanding your focus to include another person, and so on. Can you do that?

SHARON

I'm anxious to try it.

JH

Not anxious—excited.

SHARON

Right!

EXERCISES

1. Notice what feelings you experience the next time you are excited. Compare those feelings to the ones you experience prior to an important sales call or presentation. Identify the similarities and try re-labeling your pre-presentation feelings as excitement, noting how that affects your next performance.

2. Visit a crowded restaurant or coffee shop with a good friend or co-worker and try to hold a private conversation. (You may or may not want to tell your friend what you are doing.) Increase your focus on your partner until you realize you have blocked out the other conversations around you. Bring that level of intense focus to your next presentation and observe whether it lessens your anxiety.

3. Pick an upcoming meeting that you feel nervous about. Review the steps for using substitution in Chapter 8. Choose a substitution for this person that will make you feel more comfortable and perform at your best.

4. Offer to give a short presentation at a sales meeting—no more than three to five minutes. Engage someone in the group and focus exclusively on communicating with that person. When you are confidently grounded, expand your focus to include another person in your group. Continue until you have included everyone. Give yourself a hand!

THE CAST: SELLING ON YOUR FEET

13

"Improvisation is too good to leave to chance."

~Paul Simon

Sarah had spent weeks preparing her proposal showing how a growing manufacturer could consolidate its communication center, thereby improving its customer service and saving the company a considerable amount of money. All of the valuable time she had invested analyzing organizational needs, assessing the market, and projecting usage and cost savings flew out the window the moment Sarah walked into her meeting. Her client, with whom she had worked so closely, announced that the company was selling off a major part of its business and would need a much more scaled down version of her plan. And it would need the plan right away.

Sarah immediately began rescheduling the meeting, allowing herself time to come up with a new proposal, and then she saw a competitor's proposal sitting on her client's desk. Recalling the sales "improv" skills she had recently learned, Sarah quickly assessed the situation and, collaborating with her client, came up with a new version that neither Sarah or the client would have come up with on their own—a version that was a perfect fit for the company's new corporate model.

As a seller, it is virtually impossible to prepare for all of the unknowns thrown at you on a daily basis, such as a change in key decision-makers, a competitor's price cut, or a new performance requirement. To be successful now, you need to be able to quickly adapt to change with confidence and find new and innovative ways to reach your goals. In this new economy, business operates at a break-neck pace; the saying *think fast* has never been so relevant. And who thinks faster than improv performers?

Improv training is helpful for actors who work in film and television where rehearsal time can be limited or nonexistent. It also provides tools for many of the challenges salespeople face in a changing business environment, such as how to quickly establish relationships, how to adapt to change, how to pick up on subtle cues, and how to collaborate on creative solutions. By adapting three rules of improv to the business model, you will have access to a set of tools to creatively and confidently react to anything thrown your way. Except, perhaps, the odd tomato!

Three rules of improv for sellers:

1. Fire the editor.
2. Say "Yes, and...."
3. Start now.

WHY IMPROV FOR SELLERS?

"Using improv and humor to communicate in the business world is effective and powerful..."[1] ~Tom Farley, The Chris Farley Foundation

Like Sarah, I would spend hours, days, sometimes weeks preparing for an important client meeting. I would research the company, the industry, and the competition, determining how our product would best serve the client's needs. I had it all figured out before I walked in the door. Despite the careful planning, I was often met with unanticipated roadblocks. All my best laid plans, my presentation, and my proposal were suddenly as obsolete as carbon paper. Deflated, I would leave the meeting and head back to the drawing board to adapt to these changes—only to be hit yet again with something out of the blue when I walked in the door!

When I began to study improv, it was not with the intention of running off to join The Second City or perform in front of a boozy audience at the local comedy club. Improv is a recognized method for sharpening one's acting skills. I soon learned it could also be applied to many of the challenges I faced as a salesperson, where thinking on your feet is more rule than exception. What I learned from improv has helped me develop into a better scene partner and a better business partner.

In improv there is no script, no direction, and typically only the thinnest of plots. If you're in sales, this should sound very familiar to you! As a seller, how often do you walk into a situation with a thread-bare plot (an "information-gathering" meeting), unsure of what obstacles await you (objections, personality conflicts, budget cuts), or unclear about your client's needs or goals? You may be surprised to learn that, as a seller, you are already using improv!

You might be an improv seller if:

- ☆ You've ever role-played during sales training ("Okay, Bob, you be the client and I'll be the salesperson...").
- ☆ You've ever had to answer a question you weren't anticipating ("What could your company do for our new product, the Deluxe Widget?").
- ☆ You've ever walked into a meeting prepared for one client and found yourself in front of a group.
- ☆ You've ever forgotten a key prop or part of your presentation.

☆ You're ever met a potential prospect outside of business hours and had to give an impromptu pitch.

Luck may have been in your favor and it turned out well, or it may have been a dismal failure. Either way, wouldn't it be better to have a proven system that you could rely on to help you maintain control and handle any surprise with confidence?

WHAT IS IMPROV?

Have you ever marveled at how skillfully improv performers respond to the seemingly unrelated suggestions thrown at them? Though by its very nature improv is spontaneous and unscripted, there is much more to it than simply spitting out the first thing that comes to mind. There are certain commonly adhered to rules or guidelines in improv that ensure performers operate at their best and keep the action moving forward. And though it may seem quite effortless and spontaneous, improv performers put in a lot of practice in order to achieve the kind of lightning-quick speed and laser-like focus necessary to react to changing circumstances.

Improv's roots go back to the mid-1500s in Europe, when traveling troupes of performers would put on shows in public squares, improvising dialogue within a provided situation.[2] This movement, Commedia Dell'Arte, was popular for approximately 200 years, then reinvented in the 1930s by Viola Spolin, an acting teacher in Chicago, into what we recognize today as improvisation. Spolin developed a series of techniques originally designed to help actors access their creativity and self-expression, outlined in her book *Improvisation for the Theater*. It is only recently that some progressive-thinking businesses have begun using improv exercises to promote creativity and spontaneity among their employees.[3]

How many times have you left a meeting, gotten in your car, and as you pulled out of the parking lot thought, "I should have said...blah, blah!"? We are programmed as adults to edit ourselves. Some of us take that too far. Rather than risk looking foolish or saying something wrong, we end up saying nothing. We often overthink things or talk ourselves out of taking an action, getting in the way of our natural creativity and spontaneity. Improv allows you to tap into your creative voice within so that you can adjust to changing variables as they come up. It fosters honest communication by eliminating fear of failure, self-judgment, and censorship. It's an extremely valuable business tool that you can put to work in your career immediately by following the steps as outlined in this chapter.

"Do I Have to Be Funny to Use Improv?"

"Dying is easy, comedy is hard." ~Sir Donald Wolfit, British actor and director

Although improv troupes such as The Second City Comedy Improv Troupe and Upright Citizens Brigade and television shows such as *Whose Line Is It Anyway?* are usually linked with comedy, many dramatic improv scenes are as compelling to watch as any comedy. Humor is great when it works. The little-known truth about comedy is that trying too hard to be funny can fall flat. Humor is often the byproduct of being intensely focused on something. Think about some of the times you've laughed the loudest. Wasn't it often when someone was utterly and devastatingly serious? A lot of comedy is found in shared experiences and the unexpected. Improv allows you to be open to these opportunities and capitalize on them to create rapport and move the sale forward. So although you may stumble upon humor, don't get hung up on being funny as a goal. By being relaxed, receptive, open, and focused, the funny may find you.

3 Rules of "Improv" for Sellers

1. Fire your editor.

"The exciting part of acting, I don't know how else to explain it, are those moments when you surprise yourself." ~Tom Cruise

Nothing kills creativity faster than self-judgment and critique. As adults, we learn to censor ourselves and control our impulses. Most of us have an internal editor looking over our shoulder, giving us the go-ahead to speak and act only after pre-approving our content. If you've ever had a conversation with a 4-year-old child, you know what it's like not to have an editor on duty! Although we need that internal guidance system to get along socially and avoid being slapped a dozen times a day, most of us allow our editor to rule with too heavy a hand, often killing the seed of an idea before it has a chance to grow. We learn to mistrust or override our gut, think logically, weigh all the facts, and evaluate the possible reactions and pitfalls before allowing ourselves to act or respond. Some of us become afraid to change a period to a comma for fear of offending our inner editor.

Our editor is fear-based. It's a self-protective mechanism designed to help us avoid pain, embarrassment, failure, or negative outcomes of any kind. It's a defensive measure that blocks spontaneity and creativity. And the more we practice fear-based editing, the more we become dependent upon it.

When exploring options and trying to find new ways to deal with obstacles and change, it's important to give the editor living rent-free in your head the afternoon, day, or weekend off. Improv helps you to loosen the reigns on your creativity and get in touch with your untrained mind, the part that existed before you learned established patterns of thinking and acting that can often keep you trapped. Instead, learn to coexist with your inner editor and you can become more alert, aware, and insightful than you ever thought possible. Think of the times you had a first reaction or a gut feeling that you ignored. Were you sorry? Why do so many teachers recommend you go with your first answer?

Let go of your inner editor

Letting go of the editor can produce fear. As an actor, I felt comfortable getting on stage once I had memorized my lines, studied my cues, and knew what was going to take place in the scene. But "improv" strips all of that away. Security and certainty are replaced with doubt. *What if I have nothing to say? What if I make a fool of myself? What if I say something inappropriate?* Most of our fears are unfounded. We've been so successfully socialized that it's unlikely we are going to suddenly regress to the level of a naughty 4-year-old or a drunken frat boy if we let our guard down just a little bit. Strive to loosen up and let go of old thought patterns, and allow new creative ideas to flow in. In other words, fire your editor.

How to fire your editor

☆ **Don't overthink.** Notice I didn't say don't think. You know what overthinking is: going over and over something, hoping to locate new information in that great file folder in your head, waiting for a definitive red or green light from the editor. But overthinking is deadly when it comes to spontaneity and innovation. Like staring at the sun too long, if we stare at a thought too long, our vision blurs and we lose focus. Sometimes backing off from a problem and focusing on something else for a while brings new ideas bursting through—seemingly out of nowhere. Sometimes just quickening our reaction can keep us from overthinking.

☆ **Trust your first instinct.** Fear can cause us to doubt our first true thought or instinct, which could be the spark of a great new idea. Listen closely for that small voice inside and let it blossom before your inner editor steps in and crushes it. You may have kept that inner voice so tightly reigned in that, like a beaten dog, it requires coaxing to come out, and assurance that it is safe to be heard. If you learn to trust that voice and are willing to make a few mistakes, it will gradually become a working part of your thought process.

☆ **Monitor your thoughts.** Most of the time we go through the day without questioning our habitual way of thinking. If you start to place more awareness on your thoughts, becoming mindful, as the Buddhists call it, you may be surprised at how often you stop yourself or dismiss an idea before giving it a fair chance. When you notice yourself putting the brakes on an idea, ask yourself what that first glimmer of a thought or gut reaction was and why you stopped yourself.

☆ **Overcome your fear.** Your editor is trying to protect you from experiencing something painful or uncomfortable. What triggers your editor to jump in? Are you afraid of looking silly or making a mistake? Are you being overly critical of yourself? Are your fears warranted? Or are they perhaps exaggerated to keep you stuck? Ask yourself what my friend, author and comedian Diane Conway asks in her book, *What Would You Do if You Had No Fear?* Then do it.

☆ **Look for the positive.** Instead of judging your first reaction negatively, look for the positive in it—no matter how silly or insignificant it may seem. You need to create a supportive environment to encourage your inner voice to come out. Give yourself credit for recognizing your first thought and letting go of critical self-judgment.

Improv exercises and scenes are usually done at such a quick pace that your editor has less time to work, allowing your first real thought or insight to emerge before the editor can put a stop to it. Next time you are in a situation where you need to explore some new options or respond quickly, give that little editor in your head a few hours off.

2. Say "Yes, and...."

"Every interpersonal situation has a solution in which everyone wins."~Del Close, author, Improv Olympic director

Selling is a collaborative process. If you think you can *make* someone buy a product or service, you aren't thinking. You can *facilitate* a sale. You can *remove* all the obstacles to a sale. You can make the conditions *favorable* for a sale. But long-gone are the days when you were the only game in town and people had no choice but to buy from you. In today's world, you need the prospect's cooperation to sell them anything, whether it's jewelry or jet engines.

Improv performers also know that their scene partner's cooperation is vital to moving the scene forward. How do they get it? They get it by making their partner look good, being open to her ideas, respecting her perspective, and collaborating with her on new solutions; in other words, by saying yes to her. The best improvisers and sellers achieve success by putting the spotlight on their partners in a "you win/I win" game. Saying yes creates an attitude of acceptance. A common "improv" expression is *accept every offer as a gift*, no matter what your partner gives you. If she offers you a banana, you make it the best scene about a banana you can.

Improv performers take this even one step further by saying "Yes, and..." to their partners.[4] This keeps the scene moving forward, increases the number of possibilities in the scene, and keeps the lines of communication flowing. It also acknowledges and incorporates each partner's contribution to the scene. "Yes and..." does not mean you are rolling over and agreeing with whatever your partner says, but rather, you are acknowledging your partner's reality, adding your own perspective to it, and building a new reality together. Together, you become co-creators of the scene.

Don't block

The opposite of saying "Yes and...." states Keith Johnson in his pivotal book, *Impro: Improvisation and the Theater,* is blocking or denial. Denial in improv negates what one partner has established and often brings the scene to a dead stop. Notice the difference in the following two examples:

Scene One:

    Player A: What do you think of my new monkey?

    Player B: That's not a monkey. That's a dog.

Scene Two:

> Player A: What do you think of my new monkey?

> Player B: He's cute, and he looks a little bit like that one that escaped from the zoo.

In the first scene, Player B has completely shot down Player A's reality; in the second scene, Player B used "Yes, and…" to head the scene in a new and interesting direction.

Blocking can be more subtle. This is where we seem to say yes, but we are actually saying no. The quickest way to destroy a collaborative process is to argue with your prospect or dismiss his points with a *but…* Communication experts often warn that anything said before the word *but* may as well be thrown out. If you've ever received a lame apology, such as "I'm sorry I hurt your feelings, *but* you deserved it," you'll know what I mean. Notice how the seller blocks the client in the following example:

> Client: I do all my business with Company X.

> Response: Yes, *but* you've never tried our product.

This puts the client in the position of defending his decision to do business with your competitor.

Better response: "Yes, and that's the standard we measure ourselves against. What is exciting is that we have a solution that gets better results."

With "Yes, and…" you've acknowledged the client's point, as well as offered an alternative perspective without getting his defenses up. "Yes, and…" is a simple and effective tool for fostering a more collaborative relationship, whether it's with prospects, co-workers, friends, or family.

Say "Yes, and…" to Jell-O

My most challenging "Yes, and…" scenario happened as an advertising account executive for *The National Enquirer*. As you can imagine, people had very strong opinions about the publication—some deserved, some not.

I had a big meeting set with the brand managers for Jell-O at parent company Kraft's headquarters in New York. With *The Enquirer*'s readership comprised of 85 percent mothers, Jell-O seemed to be a natural advertising fit for our magazine. Halfway through my presentation, the brand manager informed me in no uncertain terms that Jell-O was not a good profile for the magazine. I asked why. Jell-O, she said, was just "too upscale" for *The Enquirer*. Though I was tempted to argue her premise that a 69-cent box of powdered gelatin could possibly be considered upscale, I remembered the "Yes, and..." rule from improv. Instead, I said, "Yes, *and* the good thing is that most people aspire to a class above themselves and the products used by that class, so in that respect, it would make great sense for Jell-O to be in our publication." She stopped and I could sense her searching for a way to dispute this before finally giving up and getting honest: She agreed with me, but there was a higher-up who "could not be named" who had a problem with a recent issue of the magazine and would never approve it as long as he signed off on the plans. I didn't get the Jell-O business that year, but the brand manager remembered me and recommended me for a Kool-aid campaign, which I did get, proving you never know where "Yes, and..." will take you!

3. Start now.

"Whatever you want to do, do it now. There are only so many tomorrows." ~Michael Landon, actor

Improv is about taking actions in the present. Not talking about what you're going to do or waiting for the perfect moment to do it. In improv, action is always preferable to non-action. And just starting anywhere within the scene is preferable to waiting. As a seller, how many times do you wait for just the right time to call a prospect, often talking yourself out of making the call? *She might be at lunch. She probably just got in and is busy checking e-mails. I bet she's getting ready to leave.* Though timing can be an important consideration, unless you know definitively that it's *not* a good time, waiting for the perfect time wastes precious time. It becomes a bad habit that quickly leads to one of a seller's worst enemies: procrastination.

Improv scenes are short and to the point. Audiences get bored if performers take too long to establish a scene, create a relationship, and start acting. And your prospect will get bored if you take too much time getting to the point as well. Attention spans are growing increasingly shorter in this fast-paced world, and if you don't jump in quickly, you will get left behind. Compare the following scenes:

Scene One:

 Bob: Hello, I'm Bob.

 Carol: Hi, I'm Carol.

 Bob: Nice to meet you.

Carol: You also.

Bob: How are you?

Carol: Great.

Bob: How are you?

Carol: I just got robbed.

Scene Two:

Carol: Can you help me? I just got robbed.

Bob: Stay here while I call the police.

Carol: No police! There's a warrant out for my arrest!

Scene Two cuts to the chase. It doesn't waste time with a lot of unnecessary set-up or a lot of meaningless pleasantries. How many sales calls do you suppose busy executives receive every day—five, 10, 20? Can you imagine listening to two or three minutes of small talk and beating around the bush before each caller gets to his or her point? If an executive takes 20 calls a day, that's one entire hour spent listening to repetitive, meaningless chatter each day! Yes, building rapport is important, but when you get a busy executive on the telephone or have just a few minutes of face-to-face time, you need to jump in and get to the interesting stuff right away. Here are two sales examples with a busy executive named Bill:

Sales example one: Jenny

Jenny: Is this Bill Miller?

Bill: Yes it is.

Jenny: Hi, Bill. This is Jenny Smith with ABC Services.

Bill: Yes?

Jenny: How are you?

Bill: Fine. And you?

Jenny: Great. I'm really enjoying the fall weather. How about you?

Bill: Yes, it's nice. What can I do for you, Jenny?

Jenny: I'd like to talk to you about your accounting needs.

Bill: What about them?

Sales example two: Pete

Pete: Bill Miller. Pete Smith with XYZ Services. I noticed you were using PDQ & Associates and wondered if they had offered you the new elite-level service.

Bill: What elite-level service?

Pete: It's brand new in the industry, and we're one of the first companies to offer it to our customers. It fully integrates your accounting system with our server, allowing you to save money and time on your billing and financial statements.

Bill: Sounds interesting. What does it cost?

Pete: If I could sit down with you and get a few quick pieces of information, I would be able to tell you pretty closely what it would cost and how much you could save. Do you have 20 minutes on Friday morning?

Bill: I guess 10 o'clock would work.

Pete simply cut to the chase by getting to the important points and eliminating the dull parts all together. This is what improv genius Del Close called "Working at the top of your intelligence and respecting the audience's intelligence."[5] In other words, trust that the audience is smart enough to understand the scene without spending a lot of wasted time setting it up. If you think about it, this is not Bill's first rodeo. He's probably taken a sales call or two before. He knows you want to sell him something and you're not likely to surprise him or catch him off guard by stalling. In fact, you're much more like to annoy him and try his patience if you take too long. Get to the point without being rude or abrupt. And don't wait. Start *now!*

A SALES PRO SCENE: "START NOW"

THE CAST

CAREY: A rep for a fitness equipment company.

MARIETTA: The manager of a popular health club.

THE SETTING

Carey's business was strong—up until the market meltdown, when health clubs and gyms across the country suddenly began cutting costs and deferring investments in new or upgraded equipment. With the pool of buyers shrinking, Carey's competition was even more aggressive about protecting their accounts, and Carey was having trouble getting an opportunity to bid on new business. Carey finally got a meeting set up with Marietta, who managed one of the few clubs in his territory planning on replacing their equipment, but his meeting got cut short.

DIRECTOR'S SCENE NOTES:

JH

What happened at your meeting with Marietta?

CAREY

She said she was really pressed for time and asked if I could talk to her while we walked through the club. I asked her about her business and told her a little bit about our line. She was very nice, but then we got interrupted by one of the managers, who needed her for something right away. She told me to call her the next day but of course she didn't return any of my calls over the next week. I finally I got an e-mail from her saying she was going to stick with her current vendor because of the economy.

JH

What's the most important point you wanted to impress upon Marietta?

CAREY

That a lot of serious gym-goers actually seek out clubs that carry our equipment.

JH

Did you communicate that?

CAREY

No. Like I said, she was really in a hurry and we got cut short.

JH

So, you were hoping for a better time to do that?

CAREY

Well, yes. A time when we could sit down and I had her full attention.

JH

And what would have been wrong with getting to the good stuff right away as you were walking through the club?

CAREY

I wanted to build some rapport by asking her some questions first. It didn't seem like the ideal time to just jump into my pitch.

JH

So instead, the *less* ideal time has passed and now you've potentially lost an opportunity because you were waiting for the *more* ideal time.

CAREY

I guess so.

JH

I bet you won't let that happen again! So let's talk about what you're going to do now. The main reason Marietta doesn't want to change is because of the economy?

CAREY

That's what she said.

JH

Is it true that keeping her current vendor will be less expensive?

CAREY

Not necessarily. It might seem like a better deal initially, but the equipment she's buying needs more service and doesn't have the life expectancy that ours does. She'd probably spend less money with our company in the end—and attract some new members out of it.

JH

So role-play with me, Carey. You be Marietta and I'll be you. *Marietta, I understand your concern about keeping costs down, and I respect that. The current economic conditions have certainly affected the membership at many of the clubs I work with. Is that true for you?*

CAREY

As a matter of fact, yes. Our renewal rate has declined and our new membership numbers are way down.

JH

Yes, and I'm sure you've got a lot of members deciding whether their membership is worth it or shopping around for the best deal, right?

CAREY

For sure.

JH

And I bet it's easier and less expensive to keep a member than to get a new one, right?

CAREY

Oh, absolutely.

JH

And that's why the clubs we've worked with have been so happy with us: Their renewal rates are higher than ever—in part because their members see that they're reinvesting in the club with the latest state-of-the-art equipment.

CAREY

That's nice, but we're really interested in getting new members.

JH

Yes, I can appreciate that, and the great thing is that these clubs have also seen a big increase in new membership among serious athletes who are familiar with our equipment line and actually seek out gyms that carry it.

CAREY

Well...

JH

Do you see what I'm doing here, Carey?

CAREY

You're turning everything I say into a positive.

JH

Right. I'm using "Yes, and..." to turn her concerns into a case for your company. Do you think you can do that?

CAREY

Yes, and I will start doing it now!

EXERCISES

1. Take the following prospect responses and respond, "Yes, and…" in as many ways as you can.

    Example: "I'm going to think about it for awhile. Let me get back to you."

    Possible response: "Yes, and I would generally recommend that. However the way these are flying off the shelves, I can't guarantee it will still be available when you're ready to move ahead. It would be safer to write it up. Is there something I didn't cover or something that made you think you should give it some more thought?"

    Now try your hand at these:

    ★ "My budget just got cut. We're going to have to table this."

    ★ "Why don't you get back to me in about six months?"

    ★ "I think we're going to go with your competitor. I'll give you a shot at our business next year."

2. Fire the editor for a day and listen to your gut rather than your head. If you're feeling confident, you may want to react with your gut as well, or you can choose to write down your gut reactions and then review them later to see how they corresponded with the situation. Remember: You may have to quicken your reaction time to outsmart your editor. Note what comes out of this experiment.

3. Tape yourself when you call a prospect. Write down word-for-word what you say, then read it back to yourself. Ask yourself how you would respond if you were on the receiving end. Now rewrite it, eliminating any filler words and moving your most important point to the beginning. Strive to cut at least 30 percent of your original verbiage.

THE CLOSING NIGHT: OBSTACLES TO CLOSING

14

"Maximum conflict is what you should be looking for. The more conflict… the more interesting the performance of the play."

~Michael Shurtleff, casting director/author, *Audition*

Ben sells shares of luxury suites at a major sporting arena with an average price tag upward of $300,000 annually. His market is a high-level corporate customer who uses these suites for entertaining major clients and rewarding company personnel. The recent focus on corporate overspending on travel and entertainment has hurt the industry, and Ben's business is suffering. When he got an appointment with the chief executive of a large corporation that had just relocated to the city, Ben went to work. He knew that his company's current strategy of trying to minimize the pressures that his clients were under when making these types of decisions had not proven effective. What was left unspoken by either the prospect or the salesperson was often the real reason behind the decision.

Ben pored through information that a corporate executive would be exposed to regarding entertainment and rewards spending. He broke the objections down into external obstacles (costs, perceived value, competitive opportunities) and internal obstacles (fear, guilt, uncertainty), and prepared himself to address each one. He calculated the value of spending three hours with an important customer at each game and treating valued employees both on a monetary level and a personal level, and compared that to other rewards' programs.

Prepared for each obstacle with a ready solution to each, Ben was able to help his new client feel good about making an important investment in client/ employee relationships.

Handling obstacles in a positive and proactive way is a culmination of all of the skills you've learned in this book: You are confident within your role and clear about your objectives. You have established rapport, presented with intention, and listened with animation. You have discovered what is important to your prospect and zoned in on the authentic urgency. Now you will learn how to combine these skills into a successful strategy for moving through obstacles to closing a sale.

Acting techniques for closing a sale:

☆ Identifying obstacles.

☆ Handling obstacles.

☆ Asking closing questions.

☆ Acting "as if."

☆ Buying against type.

☆ Taking closing actions.

IDENTIFYING OBSTACLES

A scrawny, mediocre athlete longs to play football for Notre Dame (*Rudy*). A man wrongly accused of murder spends 20 years in prison overcoming abuse, ignorance, and deception (*The Shawshank Redemption*). A poor, abused, and overweight teen finds a way out of a Chicago ghetto (*Precious*). Movies and plays are not written about people pursuing a goal with little or nothing standing in their way, and important sales are rarely made without overcoming a few obstacles. Obstacles often build up in movies until the outcome looks bleak. Just as soon as one hurdle is crossed, another one takes its place. The goal is in sight, but slips away again and again. This archetypical hero's journey keeps an audience on the edge of their seats and the greater the obstacles to overcome, the more gratifying the resolution.

Good actors welcome obstacles—even seek them out—because they know that without, them a scene is lifeless and flat. Just as in the movies, obstacles can build up in sales as well—especially if they are not addressed early on—and a satisfactory solution is not guaranteed, sellers would do well to take this lesson from actors: If there are obstacles, there is life in the scene *and* there is life in the sale.

Obstacles vs. Objections

As an actor, anything that gets in the way of getting what you want in a scene is often referred to as an obstacle. I prefer to use the term *obstacle* in sales also, in place of the more commonly used *objection*, because an objection implies an entrenched negative position, whereas an obstacle can merely be a hurdle, a hitch, or a stumbling block. It is an obstruction that has many ways to be negotiated.

Obstacles are a key element of drama, as discussed in Chapter 7. They create conflict and interest, and they are vital for keeping the audience engaged in the story, just as obstacles keep the prospect engaged in the sale. According to one study, prospects who buy have 58 percent more objections than those who don't.[1] I would much prefer to have a prospect throw out 20 obstacles than one "I don't care." But, as do most people, sellers tend to shy away from conflict because it is uncomfortable. We learn to associate it with arguing or discord, but that doesn't have to be the case. Conflict can be as simple as wanting two mutually exclusive things: You want to be a doctor, but you faint at the sight of blood. You want to have a family, but you'd also like to travel around the world.

In our attempts to avoid conflict, we often rush to smooth things over, ignoring the elephant in the room. We pretend not to notice when our client flinches at price. We gloss over the fine print in the contract that typically creates tension. We assume our prospect's silence means agreement. This head-in-the-sand strategy is as ineffective in sales as it is in other areas of life. We think that by ignoring or not acknowledging a problem that the problem will disappear. But that is magical thinking. Why not seek out obstacles as actors do and use them as an opportunity for action, for engagement, for discovery? Look at obstacles as a way to get your prospect further involved in the sales process. Deal with them as they arise so they don't build up into something insurmountable.

It is the way in which we deal—or don't deal—with obstacles that can make or break a sale. The following techniques will help you find new ways to look at obstacles and new ways to handle them like a sales pro.

Types of Obstacles

In sales, obstacles typically fall into one of three basic categories:

1. External.
2. Internal to the prospect.
3. Internal to the seller.

1. External obstacles

Most obstacles are external and therefore obvious, such as your prospect having a limited amount of time or a negative experience with your company. There's been a budget cut. A competitor has offered a better deal. It could be almost anything, but it's not enough to know what the obstacle is simply on a superficial level. Chapter 8 provides tools that can help you recognize, acknowledge, and empathize with the obstacles that your prospect faces in order to best address them.

2. Internal obstacles (prospect)

Sometimes you find yourself working with a prospect who has no objections, yet you still can't close the deal. She *seems* to be interested. She *says* there are no issues. But you cannot get a definite commitment from her. Perhaps you have not hit on what's important or established authentic urgency. Chapter 7 provides techniques for identifying where and why you may be stuck—and how to move ahead.

3. Internal obstacles (seller)

It's easy to blame the client or prospect for not closing a sale. The more difficult challenge is to recognize when the problem lies within us as sellers. Do we really know how to close? And if we do, do we actually have the persistence and courage to do it? Many sellers do the footwork brilliantly: establish rapport, qualify the prospect, identify needs, and present with intention, only to leave that crucial final step in the hands of fickle fate. *I did everything I could. I gave it my best shot.* The expectation that the close should come naturally and effortlessly just because you performed every other step correctly needs to be smashed. You must still do what many sellers do not do: break down the obstacles and specifically and persistently ask for the business.

HOW TO HANDLE OBSTACLES

Break them down.

Obstacles are easier to address and understand if we break them down, just as Ben did in our example. The key steps we learned in Chapter 6 for breaking down a script apply here as well. Focus on the intention behind the words and restate it in your own words—for your clarification and that of the prospect.

Example of obstacle break down:

Prospect: We can't afford to change vendors right now.

Seller: So your concern is strictly a financial one? (focus on intent)

Prospect: Well, yes. And we have a contract that would be hard to get out of.

Seller: So you're concerned that it's going to cost you more to switch vendors than to stay with the same one. Is that right? (restate it in your own words)

Be specific.

You need to know precisely what you want your prospects to do before you can communicate it to them. Have you answered all of the closing questions for yourself—in particular, the what, when, where, how, and how many? Often, our requests are vague: *Are you ready to buy our products?* And vague questions get vague answers. *Not yet. We'll see. I need to think about it some more.*

Details are critical for advancing the action of a scene. As an improv performer, the more details you provide, the more control you have over the direction of the scene, and the easier you make it for your partner to follow through with the scene. In sales, the more details you provide for your prospect, the easier you make it for him or her to follow through with the sale.

Example of how details advance an improv scene:

Scene 1: *I love your new, black velvet Elvis painting you hung over the waterbed! You must have one heck of a Hollywood decorator.*

As opposed to:

Scene 2: *I love the picture you picked out for the bedroom.*

In the first scene, we provided our scene partner with a lot of detailed information about our circumstances and our relationship: We are in his home, he likes kitschy things, he lives in Hollywood, and he has, possibly, hired a decorator. In the second scene, we provided our partner with minimal information. Now it is on his shoulders to fill in the details. What is the picture? Where is the house located? Who is he and what is his relationship to you?

In addition to moving the action forward, details also engage us emotionally. If you were flipping through the channels and landed on one of the two following programs already in progress, which one might you stay tuned to watch?

Program1: *I'm out of gas. Can you give me a ride?*

Program 2: *I was chased off the road by my crazy ex-boyfriend, and when my car hit the curb, my tire blew out. Can you give me a ride?*

If you think this only applies on-stage, think again. Which of the following sales scenes is more interesting and engaging?

Scene A:

Seller: Would you like to buy this car?

Prospect: I don't know. Let me think about it. (End of conversation.)

Scene B:

Seller: Would you be interested in getting a screaming deal on this 2011 BMW if you were able to trade your SUV for a price that would surprise you?

Prospect: What's the "screaming deal"? How much do you think I could get for my car? (Conversation moves forward.)

Be persistent.

It's a human tendency to give up when things get tough. And things are certainly tough in sales right now. For many of us, territories and responsibilities have increased while support staffs and services have gotten smaller or been eliminated entirely. Time is at a premium, and we grab at the low-hanging fruit, leaving the more challenging pieces in the tree to be picked by our competitors.

A widely quoted study at Notre Dame University found the following startling facts about sales persistence:[2]

☆ 44 percent of all salespeople quit trying after the first call.

☆ Another 24 percent quit after the second call.

☆ Another 14 percent quit after the third call.

☆ Another 12 percent quit trying to sell their prospect after the fourth call.

☆ 60 percent of all sales are made *after* the fourth call.

A staggering 94 percent of all salespeople quit after making four calls or less. Yet this same study reveals that 60 percent of sales are made *after* the fourth call.[3] That means being persistent and making more than four calls could increase your business by as much as 60 percent!

Ask closing questions.

The previous percentages can easily be applied to the number of closing questions we ask as well. Most salespeople probably ask one closing question and, when they get a negative response, they retreat. Some ask two; rarer still are the ones who ask three or more. Now, asking the same question four times in a row is both annoying and ineffective; however, if you use the script break down technique you will continue to hone in on the real obstacle and get closer to a solution.

Example:

Seller: Can I write that up for you today?

Prospect: I'm really not ready to make a decision.

Seller: Is there something I didn't cover, or do you have some questions or concerns?

Prospect: No. I just don't think we need it right now.

Seller: So you don't need to start saving 50 bucks a month on your electric bill right now?

Prospect: Well...that would be nice. But we really wanted to put carpeting in the basement first.

Seller: How much time do you spend in your basement?

Prospect: None right now. But we'll use it a lot when it gets carpeted.

Seller: So you probably don't have the heat on in your basement now.

Prospect: Well... no. We don't.

Seller: One thing I've found is that people's heating bills increase almost 25 percent when they add another space like that. So my quote was a little low—we'd probably save you about $75 a month.

Prospect: Hmmm. Let me look at that brochure again.

Where would you have stopped? Be honest. Would it have been after the first question? The second? The third? And yet it probably took less than a minute to ask a few additional questions. When you think about all the time you invest in planning the call, getting the appointment, and giving the presentation, isn't it worth spending a few more (perhaps uncomfortable) minutes probing for the real obstacles to increase your chances of closing by as much as 60 percent?!

Acting "As If"

Acting "as if" combines the role work we did in Chapter 2 with the Magic If in Chapter 8 to help facilitate a smoother closing. It is particularly effective when the obstacles reside within us. Next to cold-calling, closing probably brings up more fear than any other step in the sales process. Acting "as if" allows us to walk through those uncomfortable feelings and ask the tough questions. In the same way that we built our sales role in Chapter 2, acting "as if" means defining what qualities we need to feel confident in closing, and identifying where we have exhibited these qualities in other areas of our life. Then we apply these qualities to the closing situation by using the Magic If, asking ourselves, "How would I act if I had these qualities right now?" Acting "as if" helps us to assume our role with confidence and take all of the necessary closing actions despite any doubt or fear that we might be experiencing.

It is an assumptive closing technique that serves two functions: It puts us in a confident mental state, and it offers a simple, assertive way to close your prospect without putting her on the defensive. If your prospect is not ready to close, or there are still obstacles at this point, it will reveal those as well.

Steps for acting "as if"

1. Determine what qualities you need to close.
2. Discover where you exhibit these qualities in other roles in your life.
3. Decide how to apply these qualities to your role as closer.
4. Act as if you had these qualities in your current circumstances.

An acting "as if" sales example:

Jean loved hosting wine tasting parties to promote the specialty wine label she represented. She delighted in introducing a new wine to her friends and neighbors, but when it came to asking for orders, Jean could not get the words out. Using the previous steps, Jean discovered that although she lacked the confidence to close wine sales, she was extremely confident as a writing instructor at the local community college. Even though she had not studied writing, her passion for telling a story and commitment to learning the craft of writing had gotten her published in several regional magazines. In the same way, she realized that, even though she had not studied winemaking professionally, she was a dedicated student of the winery she represented and was passionate about their products and passing on a good value to her friends. At the next wine party, Jean was able to act as if she were as confident asking friends to purchase her wine as she was asking her students to complete an assignment.

Fear of "No"

Fear of closing manifests itself in not asking closing questions, creating additional steps, offering to do more research, setting more appointments—anything to prolong the sales process and avoid the possibility of hearing that dreaded word *no*. Because no matter what we are told by managers, trainers, or other sales gurus, most of us on the front line do not really believe that *the sale begins when the customer says no*. This is actually the title of a book written in 1966 before the existence of personal computers, cell phones, or social media, and when gas cost 30 cents per gallon. I think author Robert Frare summed it up best in his more recent book, *Partner Selling*: "The tricky, manipulative selling techniques of the past, such as close early and close often or the sale begins when the client says no…, no longer work—and turn everyone off, clients and sales people alike." That was written in 2000. We can now officially announce, like cheap gas, the days of never taking no for an answer are dead.

Fearing no becomes a problem when we hear no in every obstacle or stalling statement. It's as if we are listening through the ears of a child whose mother says "we'll see," which he knows really means "no." Responses such as "I'm not sure," "Call me after the holidays," and "I'm happy with my competitor" are *not* the type of no's that should stop a sale. These are obstacles. I worked with one buyer who had a sign over her desk that read: *What part of No don't you understand?* It's important as a seller to understand when no means no, and when it means you simply have more work to do.

Casting Against Type

Actors often get typecast into certain kinds of roles, whether leading ladies, bad guys, or comic relief. When an actor gets cast in something that is completely different than the roles we expect to see them in, it's referred to as *casting against type*.

In *Tropic Thunder*, leading man Tom Cruise plays a fat, bald, egomaniacal producer. In *Natural Born Killers*, Rodney Dangerfield plays Juliette Lewis's abusive father. In *Training Day*, perennial good guy Denzel Washington wins an Oscar for playing a bad cop.

Buying Against Type

Buyers can also get typecast. When a buyer makes a purchase that is completely different than what we expect him to buy, I call this *buying against type*. Many times sellers don't close because *they* aren't certain that their product or service is right for a particular prospect or *they're* not convinced that the prospect wants or needs it. It's as if we step in and play casting director for our prospects. But how would you like to be the casting director that held Denzel Washington back from an Oscar-winning performance? In cases like this, we need to open our minds and expand our idea of what may be right for our client, because ultimately we never really know what's going on inside another person. We may make every effort to address that person's concerns, ask probing questions, listening with intent, and reading his body language, but in the end, we can never fully know someone else. Don't let your preconceived ideas keep you from moving forward with a prospect that may be perfectly ready and willing to close.

I learned a lot about buying against type when I was selling residential real estate, in which people frequently surprise you with their choices. I was helping a good friend find a new condo and, as she and I shared similar background and tastes, it was almost as if I was looking for a place of my own. I dragged her to every new condo building in town. But while I got very excited about each one—gushing about the building amenities, the fantastic views, the shiny new kitchens, and hardwood floors—she remained uncharacteristically subdued, despite the fact that these were all the features she claimed to want in a new home.

Two weeks into our search, we drove by a boxy little run-down house with a For Sale sign in the yard and my friend asked if we could look at it. Questions formed in my mouth: *This old house? On this busy street? But you want a condo!* But I swallowed my words and set up a showing. When we walked through the house, I could see that it had a certain charm, but still there was the old kitchen with the chipped countertops and avocado appliances, the warped floors and peeling wallpaper, the overgrown yard, and the sagging driveway. It was hard to keep my thoughts to myself as my friend quietly walked through, taking in every nook and cranny, opening every door and cabinet.

When we drove off, I steered toward the next condo on the list, when I realized I had not asked her my normal post-showing questions. "How do you feel about the house? How does it compare to everything you've seen so far?" She paused for a long moment, staring out the window, before turning to me with resolve and saying "I'd like to put in an offer on it." I nearly drove off the road. I had no idea my friend had the ability to see potential in such disrepair. I didn't know that her father had been a contractor and growing up she enjoyed going along with him to his projects and watching something new and wonderful emerge from the shamble.

I learned an important lesson from that experience: Don't typecast your prospect. Never assume something is or isn't right for someone else. Ask the closing questions even if you're not sure.

TAKING CLOSING ACTIONS

Once you know what is in your way (the obstacle) you must ask yourself how you are going to get around, under, or over it. In Chapter 5, we talked about motivation and the importance of choosing an active verb to get what we are fighting for. Obstacles provide us another opportunity to choose an active verb to take action. People typically deal with obstacles in one of three ways:

1. They give up on their goal.

2. They change their goal.

3. They find a way around the obstacles.

Most of us have a baseline reaction that we fall back on subconsciously. Too many of us don't realize that we have a choice. But you are a conscious closer now, and are able to pause and consider the given circumstances and your relationships before deciding on the appropriate action.

Take a look at a partial list of closing actions and find one or two that spark a new attitude or different energy and test it out. For example, how would you *assume* the business as opposed to *asking* for it like you always do?

Closing action verbs

ask	appeal	assume	assure	attract	beckon	cajole	captivate
charm	claim	clamor	coax	counsel	direct	emphasize	encourage
encourage	endorse	entice	entreat	excite	expect	expedite	guide
hypothesize	incite	infer	insist	inspire	instigate	invite	lead
persuade	petition	press	rally	request	rouse	seek	solicit
spur	stir	sway	tempt	test	testify	urge	whet

EXERCISES

1. Determine what obstacle is keeping you from closing a sale and whether it is external, internal to the buyer, or internal to you.

2. Break down the obstacle into its basic components and put it in your own words.

3. Answer the following closing questions for yourself: what, where, when, how, and how many?

4. Develop two detailed closing questions for this obstacle. For example:

   Obstacle: We're happy with our current supplier.

   Response 1: So you are confident that your current supplier, PDQ Automotive, can continue to provide you with the same level of service?

   Response 2: Many of our clients thought they were happy with their supplier also until they realized they were not getting the additional tools we offer through our executive service program. Are you aware of what you're missing?

ACT IV:
The Encore

THE CALLBACK: GENERATING REPEAT BUSINESS

15

"An actor entering through the door, you've got nothing. But if he enters through the window, you've got a situation."

~Billy Wilder, director

Barry is an agent with a well-known national insurance company that of-fers competitive life and disability insurance plans for individuals and families. Barry keeps up on the latest industry news and has a good rapport with his clients. However, his sales numbers have hit a frustrating plateau. When Barry's manager Dana attends a client meeting with him, she points out afterward that Barry is not taking strong enough steps to get a firm commitment from his client to provide referrals. Barry is uncomfortable with Dana's suggestions and fears this aggressive behavior will shut the door on future business altogether.

Barry and I work out a referral plan using the same steps actors use for securing an agent (described in this chapter), which allows Barry to ask for a specific commitment from his clients without feeling pushy or appearing ag-gressive. The first meeting after Barry tries this new technique results in two qualified leads and one new client.

Generating repeat and referral business can make the difference be-tween just a good year and a really great year, yet many sellers continue to pursue this sort of business with the same tools they use to win regular busi-ness. There are also those who are hesitant to push their luck and ask for more business for fear of losing what they already have. Actors learn that in order to get bigger roles, they have to take bigger risks. To stand out, actors must be exciting and unpredictable. They have to get their best performance out of even the most mundane of scene partners or scripts. Once you learn these tools, you will never again let an opportunity for repeat or referral business pass you by. Study the mysterious quality that attracts us to particu-lar popular actors and you will learn how to multiply your business.

Acting techniques for multiplying business:

☆ Use unpredictability to your advantage.

☆ Turn a small sale into a bigger sale.

☆ Build a fan club with referrals.

☆ Make your client your agent.

UNPREDICTABILITY

"Consistency is the death of good acting." ~Michael Shurtleff

What makes some actors so compelling to watch, so interesting that you would pay to see them in anything? Certain actors have the ability to sur-prise us over and over again. Think of Johnny Depp, Robert Downey Jr., or

Tilda Swinton. They are not your average pirate, superhero, or ambitious attorney. They take on what might otherwise be rather ordinary roles and transform them into something unforgettable. How do they do it? They look for interesting choices. They are specific rather than general. And they often do the opposite of what is expected. An audience who is just waiting to be intrigued, surprised, and shaken up will go see them again and again.

Your client or prospect is also an audience waiting to be shaken up and surprised. What are you doing to make that happen? Where is the intrigue, the suspense in hearing the same pitch in the same way time and time again? As sellers, we program buyers to know exactly what we are going to say and exactly how we are going to say it. They know we will call every two weeks, every month, every quarter. And they are ready for us, ready to put us off for another two weeks, month, or quarter. They know they are not missing a must-see performance. If they think they already know everything they need to about you and your business, why would they need to see you again? What's in it for them?

Unpredictability creates curiosity; it gets your call taken, gets you in the door. It turns an "I don't have time to talk to you about that again" into "I wonder what he has to say?" Unpredictability can be a winning tactic in acting and in sales, and it sets you apart from the crowd. Let the other sellers call every other Tuesday at 2 p.m. with the same tired pitch. You can become the sales equivalent of a Johnny Depp or a Tilda Swinton—a salesperson whose performance is not to be missed.

How to Become Unpredictable

Do the routine thing in a new way

When Marlon Brando auditioned for *The Godfather*, he decided that his character had been shot in the mouth and therefore stuffed it with cotton, creating his legendary mumble.[1] It wasn't in the script. It wasn't in the direction. It's something he thought up all on his own—and you can bet he was the only actor to do that.

Should you fill your mouth with cotton on your next sales call? No, but you can break up your routine. If you always meet at your client's office, ask him to meet you at the coffee shop in his building. If you always give a 20-minute pitch, next time start out with a Q&A, or bring in a guest speaker.

Do the opposite of what is expected

Good actors often make choices that are the opposite of what the script seems to call for—and what nine out of 10 actors will do during an audition. If the line they are asked to read seems pleasant, they may deliver it in a gruff, aggressive manner. If the stage directions call for them to enter a room, they may forego the door and come through the window, as director Billy Wilder proposed. In sales, think about what everyone else does in the same situation and determine what the opposite tact would be. For example, if a prospect is typically bombarded by sellers at the outset with reasons why their product or service is better than the competition, try pointing out the positives about your competitors from the start. If common practice in your industry is to convince a customer to buy on the spot, why not tell them you will not allow them to make a purchase that day?

Fight the conventional take

Comedian T.J. Miller auditioned twice for the movie *Yogi Bear* with no luck. Refusing to give up, he filmed himself goofing around with a real 600-pound bear. The tape found its way to the chairman of Warner Brothers,who gave Miller the role.[2] Although wrestling a bear to win business may be going a bit too far, taking a step outside of the conventional in small ways, such as giving your prospect the chance to set the agenda or asking multiple-choice questions, will still set you miles apart from your competition.

Demonstrate your range

Many actors make safe choices, letting us see the same side of them over and over, such as Adam Sandler in one light comedy after another. Few actors have shown the kind of range that Christian Bale has, from disturbing films such as *American Psycho* and *The Machinist*, to cult classics like *Batman*, and most recently playing Mark Wahlberg's emaciated, drug-addicted brother in *The Fighter*.

Are your clients only seeing one side of you? The more unique facets you can show of yourself, the more interesting and memorable you become. I used to keep my acting and selling lives separate, until I realized that I was denying my clients the chance to get to know my other side. When I became more open about my interests and experience, it allowed them to become more open with me as well. It created avenues for conversation and interaction that I couldn't have imagined. Suddenly I wasn't just another salesperson. I was their connection to local theater, their go-to person for insider gossip, movie reviews, and even tickets to their favorite shows.

THERE ARE NO SMALL SALES, ONLY SMALL SALESPEOPLE

How many times have you gotten a small slice, or even a crumb of business when you were hoping for the whole pie? What did you do after you finished complaining to anyone who would listen about how much time you wasted, what a huge mistake the client made, and how your competitor didn't deserve the business? Did you sullenly write up the sale or go through the motions of fulfilling the order? Did you send it down to shipping without so much as an instruction to "handle with care" or "deliver by__"? Were you visibly impatient, ready to be done with this customer, and move on to a more promising prospect? Or did you treat the client and his small piece of business as the larger future business opportunity that it was?

Making a Big Deal Out of Small Business

One Christmas, I had to find a tiny charm for my niece that was only carried at certain jewelry stores. They were all located in malls packed with holiday shoppers, and I had to go to three before I could find even one person to help me. At my final stop, I got passed around to several salespeople before a young guy named Chad waited on me. He listened attentively, then, instead of abruptly throwing the tray of charms out in front of me and tapping his fingers until he could move on to the next Rolex buyer, he spent 15 minutes helping me find just the right charm, even calling around to other stores to see if they had it in stock. Chad was so helpful that I felt guilty not buying anything more than an inexpensive trinket from him and swore that the next time I had to buy a gift I would seek him out. Two months later, I happily went back to Chad to purchase a wedding gift, a beautiful and expensive crystal bowl.

There are no small roles, only small actors.

No matter how small the roles, good actors make the most of then. They make these roles their own with a look, a line, a delivery—putting their mark on it, and in the process, often making their performances more memorable than the main characters'. Think of Alec Baldwin in *Glengarry Glen Ross* (if you're in sales, and you haven't seen this: for shame! See a list of other not-to-miss sales movies in the Appendix.) "Coffee is for closers!" Baldwin shouts as the sales manager from hell in a seven-minute David Mamet monologue, which is his most downloaded performance on YouTube.[3] Think of Dame Judi Dench as Elizabeth I in *Shakespeare in*

Love. She made the most of less than eight minutes of screen time, and earned an Oscar for Best Actress in a Supporting Role.[4]

Creating Recurring Business From a Small Sale

Sometimes an actor gets a small role on television and is able to parlay it into a recurring or even regular role. Recurring characters usually start out as a guest star on a television series and then continue to be written into future episodes if they add something new to the show, make the other characters look good, or receive enough positive feedback. Many actors have broken out this way. Kelsey Grammer was initially cast in just six episodes of *Cheers*, but turned into a regular member of the cast and went on to star in the wildly popular spin-off, *Frasier*.[5] *Friends'* fans can't forget Chandler Bing's annoyingly nasal girlfriend, Janice, played by Maggie Wheeler, who was originally cast in a single episode and ended up appearing on 19 episodes spanning 10 seasons of the popular television series.[6] January Jones read for the role of Peggy on *Mad Men*, but creator Matthew Weiner didn't think she was right for it. He asked her to return and read for Betty Draper, a role he hadn't fully developed at the time. He promptly went home and wrote some scenes for her, making January an integral character in the show.[7]

What makes some actors one-hit wonders whereas others return season after season, even starring in their own spin-offs? It comes down to three things:

1. They add something important (*value*).
2. They stand out from the crowd (*uniqueness*).
3. They make the other characters look good (*likability*).

We've talked at length about bringing something of value and standing out from other sellers in earlier chapters, but how do you make the other character, your prospect, look good—and why should you, especially if he's just thrown you a bone?

Making Your Prospect Look Good

Many great actors credit their scene partners with making them look good. Good scene partners are generous and always looking out for their partners' best interests. Is it altruistic? Maybe. But making your scene partner look good makes for a better scene—which makes you look good as well. When actors get a weak scene partner, they often cry: "He's not giving me anything to work with!" And it's true. When one actor is not pulling his weight, it can drag down the entire scene. But if you have a weak scene partner (prospect), you have to *find* something to work with in order to create a winning sales scene.

Acting example

Mario's scene partner, Jana, reads her lines mechanically without any emotion or feeling and barely looks at Mario when he's speaking. Mario knows the scene is going to bomb if something doesn't change. Instead of getting frustrated and complaining to the rest of the cast about what a terrible scene partner he's stuck with, Mario goes to work on making it the best performance he can by:

☆ Inviting Jana to run lines outside of rehearsal in a less-pressured environment.

☆ Introducing a prop to draw Jana's attention outward and bring more life to the scene.

☆ Building on what she is doing right and suggesting ideas that would make it "even better" based on what she uniquely brings to the scene.

Sales example

Your client is buying the base product you sell: no bells, no whistles, no guarantees of more business. Though you're grateful for the business, based on previous experience, you know she's not going to be happy with it and will be back in six months to purchase an upgrade, or worse, go to your competitor. What do you do?

☆ Schedule a follow-up service in two weeks to make sure any problems she encounters are addressed early and within the warranty period.

☆ Offer a free trial of the upgrade so she can experience the difference.

☆ Congratulate her on her product choice and suggest that based on her unique needs, the upgraded model would be even better.

BUILDING A FAN CLUB WITH REFERRALS

When I talk about attracting fans, many salespeople look at me as if I'm crazy. But celebrities are not the only ones who can have fans. Fans are devotees, enthusiasts, or admirers. If you are doing business in a responsible, customer-centric way, you should be continually building a loyal fan base. Fans are your number-one source for referrals. Most of us are not maximizing that opportunity because we are not looking at it from the fan's perspective. What celebrity fans have that your fans do not are clubs offering a variety of perks and privileges for being a member. Take a look at the following fan club benefits and see how you might use them to strengthen and grow your fan base.

Fan Club Benefits

Meet and greet

The opportunity to rub elbows with their favorite celebrities is a huge draw for many fans. It allows them to learn more about the object of their fandom outside of their normal venue, and provides them with access to exclusive events to which they ordinarily would not be privy.

Although it's unlikely that you have that kind of drawing power, you can arrange to bring in industry experts who hold interest for your prospects, and who they might not otherwise have the opportunity to meet.

That special feeling

One of the greatest benefits of being in a fan club is that you feel special, everything is made easier. You get special advance notice on upcoming events, shows, or appearances. You get a special pass so you don't have to wait in line. You get special and better seats or a discount on ticket prices. Not only do you feel special, but you get to avoid the hassle that the general public must go through.

As a seller, you too can offer your fans special benefits: advance tickets to industry events, special seating, or discounts. Even if you have to buy the tickets yourself, saving clients from inconvenience and making them feel special will go a long way toward developing a devoted fan.

Exclusively yours

Where else can you find out about your favorite celebrities' latest thoughts, works, or hair color, see exclusive behind-the-scenes videos, or read their book club recommendations? Fans love to feel like they are in the know, and fan sites and newsletters provide them easy access to up-to-the-minute information.

Prospects, too, like to be in the know on their industry and their competition. If you can provide exclusive content that keeps them informed and interested, you can make your Website, e-zine, newsletter, or tweets an indispensable part of their daily reading.

Mix and mingle

Fan clubs offer an opportunity to mingle with other like-minded individuals. Websites have helped fan clubs expand exponentially because of the ease of membership and the ability to talk to other fans across the globe.

Your prospects may also enjoy the opportunity to discuss how your product or service is working for them and find out other users' experiences and recommendations as well. Look at your Website from a client's perspective: It should be user-friendly, informative, and easy to interact with like-minded clients.

Party on!

Special "fan-only" events create a sense of exclusiveness that shows appreciation for their membership. They give fans an opportunity to meet other fans and share valuable information or tips at a special event just for them.

You can host a special fans-only event, whether it's a party, a luncheon, or a field trip, to thank your prospects for their loyalty and business. This gives your clients an opportunity to network within or outside of their industry, as well as talk about how fantastic you are!

Sales fan club example:

Marilyn, a successful broker in Denver, rents out a popular restaurant and hosts an annual Christmas party for several hundred clients and potential clients. During the past eight years, the guest list has grown from 70 to 300. Costs have multiplied accordingly, but it has quickly become one of the most desired invitations of the season and is talked about all year. The party is Marilyn's primary event to market herself and though she spends more than 20 percent of her net income on it, she estimates that her business grows by at least 25 percent each year due to referrals that come directly from it. Not surprisingly, she is the top broker in her office this year. None of this would be effective if she didn't do everything else right, which she does, but it sets her apart from the crowd, giving her an edge, of which other brokers only dream.

YOU GOTTA GET AN AGENT!

It's much easier to get a role when you have a talent agent working for you. And it's much easier to get referrals when you have a client who acts as an agent for you. A good talent agent has the right contacts and knows which parts are being cast and when. Agents get what's called "a breakdown" from casting directors specifying what they're looking for in each role, such as: *Male, 6'0+, 25–30, muscular with martial arts experience*;

or *Hispanic female in her early 40s. Must speak Spanish and have own car.* The agent will search through the list of actors he represents and pick out the ones he is most confident will fit the bill. Typically the agent gets a limited number of slots so he has to pick his top candidates for each role. The agent then calls the actor and sets up the audition, makes sure he gets a copy of the script, and fills the actor in on any specific requirements of the role.

A client can act as your agent as well by introducing you to her contacts—other business professionals in her industry, or friends and associates who could potentially use your product or services. Although your client may not get anything as specific as "a breakdown" of what she is looking for, if she is involved in her industry or does any networking at all, she will have an idea of who else might be a good fit. Just like a talent agent, once your client finds out the needs of an associate or friend, she will go through her internal files and think of the top candidate(s) she can recommend with confidence. The client may an introduction and provide you with details on the prospect and his company, which could help you better target your message and may even get you an appointment. Or you could do it yourself.

Selling Without an Agent.

Without an agent, actors are left to their own resources, sending headshots and resumes out to casting directors, scouring the Internet and industry publications such as *Backstage* for audition notices. When I first moved to New York, I must have sent out a hundred headshots before getting one audition—to play a dead body on *Law & Order* (a role that, by the way, I did not get). When I did finally get an agent, it opened up doors I didn't even know were there, not to mention saved me a lot of money in postage. Suddenly I was in the running for a spokesperson on national commercials and corporate industrial films, a fitness instructor on *New York Undercover*, and Miranda's sister-in-law on *Sex & The City*—roles I would never have had a chance at without an agent recommending me to the casting director.

If you don't have a client working for you as your agent, you will be resigned to doing all of the footwork yourself as well: mass-mailings, e-mail blasts, cold-calling. Wouldn't it be nice to have someone working behind the scenes to promote you to her network so that you can focus on getting more new business? If you can find a client to represent you, someone who knows what business is available, makes the contact for you, provides you with the details, even recommends you to the decision-maker, you can consider yourself one of the fortunate few. The steps for getting your client to be an agent for you are not that much different from how an actor goes about getting an agent.

Make Your Client Your Agent.

It's not always easy to land an agent. In fact, it can seem next to impossible for new actors, primarily because they are unproven. Agents like to know that actors are working before they send the actors out. After all, agents are staking their reputations on these actors. They need to know that these actors will show up and deliver. It can be difficult to get a client to act as your agent if you are just starting out as well because your client will also be staking his reputation on you. But by following these steps, you will greatly enhance your odds of getting a client to open doors for you, doors that you didn't know even existed.

Decide what you want in an agent

There are many types of talent agents; some focus exclusively on the theater, others on film and television, and others specialize in commercials. You must be clear on what type of work you want to do. Be specific about what you want so you can be specific with your clients. The more specific you are, the easier you make their job. If you are a real estate broker, asking a client to recommend you to his friends is very different from asking him to recommend you to someone who may be getting married, having a child or moving in or out of the city in the next year. The latter prompts him to think of people who might have an upcoming need to move that may not have otherwise occurred to him.

Do your research

You need to know whether you are asking the right person for the right recommendation. If an actor tells a film agent that he really wants to be on Broadway, the agent is going to know the actor didn't do his research and throw his headshot in the wastebasket before he gets in the elevator. As an actor, you want an agent who has the right contacts for you. As a seller, you want to approach a client who has the right contacts for your product or service. Look up associations or groups of which your client is a member. Let him know which of his associates is a good fit for you and why. Make it easy for your client to represent you.

Keep working

The truth is work begets work. If a client sees that you are working hard, gaining new clients, and creating more business, she will feel more confident recommending you to others. Keep clients informed of your activities, and pass on success stories about you and your company.

Ask

You'd be surprised how many actors just assume they can't get an agent so they don't try. *I don't have enough experience or credentials. I'm only right for very specific roles.* After you have provided excellent service is the best time to ask your client if he would refer you to his friends and associates.

Do amazing work

Not average work. Not occasionally amazing work. Do amazing work every time. Overdeliver. Return calls or e-mails immediately. Don't let a second of doubt creep into your client's brain. You've done the hard part of winning the business; don't blow it on the follow-through, or you can count out any referral business.

Be reliable

Agents want to know that if they send an actor out on an audition that she is going to show up prepared and on time. Their reputations are on the line and so is yours. So don't treat a referral lightly and assume it's okay to cancel if something more definite comes up.

Don't oversell yourself

If you can't speak Latvian or deliver your product in 24 hours, don't say that you can and hope you'll be able to pull it off. If you don't live up to your selling promises, you will not only look bad, but you'll make your client look bad as well and are unlikely to get more business from them, much less another referral.

Say thanks!

Because it is an agent's job to get an actor work, many actors feel they shouldn't have to thank their agents if they get a role—and certainly no thanks are needed if they don't get the role. But most agents will tell you that, all things being equal, the actor who shows gratitude for getting sent out is more likely to be sent out again than someone who acts as if it's expected. So don't forget to show appreciation to your client for the referral—even if nothing comes from it. *Especially* if nothing comes from it.

You want to make sure that the client doesn't feel like he's wasting both his and your time by reinforcing the message that you want him to continue sending referrals and that you don't expect each one to work out.

EXERCISES

1. Pick out one sales tactic that you routinely do and figure out three ways you can make it unpredictable.

2. Target a customer or client that has given you a small sale and determine how you can make that customer look good.

3. Start a fan club. Pick one thing from the steps on how to build a fan club (meet-and-greet, pre-ticket sales, exclusive content, or party) and commit to making it happen.

4. Select a client who would be a good agent for you. Write out specifically what you can offer his network and what you are looking for in a referral. Ask him for a specific referral and show gratitude when he follows through.

THE DIRECTOR: COLLABORATING ON A WINNING PERFORMANCE

16

"The director is simply the audience. . . . His job is to preside over accidents."

~Orson Welles

Greg was excited when he got a new position as a group sales agent for a world-class resort in Vail, Colorado. However, his excitement was short-lived. Although he had a successful track record in the industry, Greg's new manager, Madelyn, was constantly looking over his shoulder, micro-managing him as if he were a rookie. Even after three months, Greg still received calls from Madelyn several times a day and was expected to run every proposal by her for approval. Greg was growing increasingly frustrated. He even began questioning his decision to leave his previous employer, where he had enjoyed a lot more autonomy. Then Greg made the connection that his new manager was playing the role of a demanding director, trying to get Greg to fall in line with her vision.

Greg realized he would first need to clarify and understand Madelyn's vision to earn her trust. Madelyn wanted Greg to deliver a high-quality message consistent with the resort's standards while proactively pursuing new business opportunities. Greg realized he was better off collaborating with Madelyn than fighting with her. Instead of waiting for Madelyn to call him, Greg began to check in with her throughout the day via text or e-mail. Instead of finishing a proposal and waiting to run it by Madelyn, Greg began to schedule a time to go over it with her and get her input from the beginning. Soon, Madelyn grew to trust that Greg shared her vision. Although still more controlling than Greg's previous manager, Madelyn started to loosen up the reigns, giving Greg some welcomed independence.

In projects where the actor and director are at odds, the end results are rarely successful. Famous examples of this are Tom Cruise and Stanley Kubrick in *Eyes Wide Shut* (Cruise developed an ulcer after nearly two years of filming with Kubrick[1]), Val Kilmer and John Frankenheimer in *The Island of Doctor Moreau* (Frankenheimer said of the experience: *"There are two things I will never do in my life. I will never climb Mount Everest, and I will never work with Val Kilmer again."*[2]), and Megan Fox was released from the *Transformers* series after fighting with director, Michael Bay.[3] It's not surprising that most of these mismatched pairs quickly part ways. Actors need to find a way to work with their directors. Though their styles may be at odds, they are ultimately working toward the same goal: getting the best possible performance out of the actor. Professional actors can't afford to waste time whining about how unfair or mean the director is or how he cut their lines. It is the actor's job to lose, not the director's. Instead, smart actors focus on how they can adjust *their* style to work with the director.

Just as a director's style may not be a good fit for every actor on the set, your sales manager's style may not be a natural fit for every member of the sales team. How actors work with directors provides a good study in how to foster a collaborative relationship with even the most challenging management types. In this chapter, we will explore techniques used by actors to create a successful working relationship with their directors, and apply them to relationships with our sales managers.

Acting techniques for a winning relationship:

☆ Understanding the manager's role.

☆ Handling a difficult manager.

☆ Identifying and working with different types of managers.

☆ Learning how to take direction.

THE DIRECTOR'S ROLE VS. THE MANAGER'S ROLE

The director is responsible for the success of the entire production—just as your manager is responsible for the success of the entire sales team, and perhaps even the company. Consider the many things on a director's plate: temperamental actors, demanding producers, unreliable crews, faulty props, tight budgets, and impossible time lines. It can make the actor's job seem downright simple. The same schedule of demands is true for sales managers. They have deadlines, production goals, support staff, and training, to mention just a few. It is important to be aware of how and where you fit into the picture.

The sales manager's role is very much like that of the director's. Sales managers are expected to provide feedback, coaching, mentoring, and encouragement. But it is during the rehearsal process, particularly in theater, that the director/actor relationship can offer valuable lessons for sellers and managers.

The Rehearsal Process

After casting a show, a director's primary function is to provide the actor with guidance as she starts to develop her role, explore relationships with the other characters, and carry out the theme of the playwright. The director gives—and the actor expects to receive—a steady stream of feedback on her progress. Together, the actor and director join forces until the show is on its feet to create a top-notch performance that the actors can re-create night after night. Rehearsal can last anywhere from a few hours or weeks in film to as many as 12 weeks in the theater. During most of my stage productions, the director gave notes or feedback until opening night. After that, I was on my own, although the director was typically available if problems arose during the run.

During the rehearsal process, all good directors foster an atmosphere in which you can grow. They allow you the opportunity to experiment without fear. They are leaders who help you find your way through blocks and make strong choices. They build strong ensembles working toward a common goal. Ideally, this is what your sales manager should provide you as well. If not, don't worry. This chapter will give you tools to handle the most challenging of manager/seller relationships.

Examples of Good Directors

Elia Kazan, co-founder of the famous Group Theater and the Actor's Studio in New York, was credited with drawing out great performances from actors such as James Dean, Natalie Wood, Karl Malden, Warren Beatty, Marlon Brando, and dozens more.[4] In his autobiography, *Songs My Mother Taught Me,* Marlon Brando describes Kazan's working style as follows:

"I have worked with many movie directors—some good, some fair, some terrible. Kazan was the best actors' director by far of any I've worked for...the only one who ever really stimulated me, got into a part with me and virtually acted it with me...he chose good actors, encouraged them to improvise, and then improvised on the improvisation.... He gave his cast freedom and...was always emotionally involved in the process and his instincts were perfect."[5]

Actress Terry Moore (*Come Back Little Sheba*) said about Kazan: "He made you feel better than you thought you could be."[6] Anthony Franciosa (*A Face in the Crowd*) explains how Kazan encouraged his actors: "He would always say, 'Let me see what you can do. Let me see it. Don't talk to me about it.' You felt that you had a man who was completely on your side.... He gave you a tremendous sense of confidence...."[7]

Eli Wallach described what made John Huston (*The Good, the Bad and the Ugly*) one of the best directors he'd ever worked with: "He didn't say, 'You have to do it this way or that way or move this way. Impress me." Eli reunited with another highly respected director, Client Eastwood, for a one-day shoot during the filming of *Mystic River.* As Eli tells it, once on set, Clint said: "How are you, Eli?" he replied, "Good." Clint said, "You ready?" Eli said, "Yeah." Clint said, "So *do* it."[8]

Unfortunately, the Clint Eastwoods, the Elia Kazans, and the John Hustons are few and far between. So what do you do when your manager has a style that doesn't jive with yours, or is just downright difficult?

WORKING WITH DIFFICULT MANAGERS

"I never said all actors are cattle, what I said was all actors should be treated like cattle." ~Alfred Hitchcock

Some famous directors are (or were) notoriously difficult to work with—Alfred Hitchcock, Stanley Kubrick, and Oliver Stone, to name a few. James Cameron, often referred to as the "scariest man in Hollywood," scoffed at Kate Winslet's claim that working with him on *Titanic* was "an ordeal" after nearly drowning and chipping a bone in her elbow, calling it nothing but "a little sputtering and coughing."[9]

But because they so often deliver amazing results, actors continue to line up to work with some of these challenging types. Most salespeople I know have had the experience of working with at least one sales manager whose primary goal seemed to be making their job more difficult. Those managers pretend to know it all, make unrealistic demands, resist new ideas, insist it's their way or the highway, and tell you what to do and how to do it.

There's a plethora of advice available on how to deal with difficult salespeople and difficult customers, but surprisingly little on how to deal with a difficult sales manager. The advice Website *Ehow.com* sums up the prevailing theory from the managers perspective, "Salespeople are notoriously difficult to manage. They hate details and paperwork, and they avoid sales managers like the plague. Good sales managers maximize the productivity of their salespeople in spite of these challenges." Wow. With this kind of a perception it's no wonder some managers treat us like naughty children!

As frustrating as a difficult manager can be to work with, you must try to keep the lines of communications open, because ultimately your performance is at stake. Like the actor, you are the one the audience sees, not your manager. The actor has to do what he can to work with his director, no matter how he feels about him or her. He has to see if there is anything he can work with, if there is something to be learned. It makes no sense to fight with the person who has the power to fire you.

Early in my career, I worked for a manager who regularly blew up in sales meetings. He would throw chairs, belittle individual sellers for poor numbers, and threaten mass firings. This same man might suddenly appear in your cubicle, inquiring about your family or handing you tickets to sporting events. In my short time there, I found that the best way to handle his volatile side was to treat him as I would any mentally unstable individual. I would give him a wide berth and mind my own business as I quietly sent my resume around the market.

Fortunately, most managers are not this extreme. There are as many styles of directing as acting, and as many styles of managing as there are selling. However, there are some characteristics and "types" common to both industries. See if you can identify your manager or a manager you have worked with in the past in the following profiles.

TYPES OF DIRECTORS AND SALES MANAGERS

The Auteur Director

Popular in the 1950s, the auteur director's "vision" and ability to create a mood or message is given more importance than the individual actors themselves. Often the director's name becomes as well-known as his or her movies, as in Orson Welles's *Citizen Kane*. Modern-day directors who might be considered auteurs are Woody Allen, Darren Aronofsky (*Pi, The Wrestler*), and David Fincher (*Fight Club, The Social Network*).

The Auteur Manager

This manager has a vision, and if you work for her, you will be expected to fulfill it. With an auteur manager, there is no mistaking that you are on *her* sales team and not flying solo. Auteur managers like to control every aspect of the "picture." They are interested in all the fine print. They may want to be copied on every correspondence to ensure that you are delivering a consistent message, or they may wish to be involved in every aspect of client negotiations and interaction. Although auteurs can be rigid, they do often respect originality in others as long as it falls in line with their vision. Think of Mel Brooks's work with Gene Wilder, or Woody Allen and Diane Keaton.

Suggestions for working with auteur managers

Identify their vision by observing and asking questions. Appeal to their concept by making it easy for them to connect what you are doing to their goal. If they are confident that their directorial vision and message is being properly communicated, as Greg did in our example, you may be given more independence.

The Demanding Director

Stanley Kubrick (1928–1999) one of history's greatest directors (*2001: A Space Odyssey, A Clockwork Orange, The Shining*) was also considered one of the most demanding. Working for Kubrick often meant giving up your personal life until the film was completed. As his former assistant Andrew Birkin said, "You don't work with Kubrick, you work for Kubrick!"[10] His projects could last several years, and his perfectionism on the set reportedly led to nervous breakdowns and ulcers: While making *The Shining,* Kubrick asked actress Shelley Duvall to do 127 takes of one scene. Kubrick made the elderly Scatman Crothers redo a seemingly unremarkable scene 148 times (a world record). At one point, Crothers became so exasperated that he broke down and cried, "What do you want, Mr. Kubrick?!"[11]

The Demanding Manager

Daily call sheets, weekly account status meetings, and lost business reports are some of the details required in sales these days that can make every manager seem like a demanding tyrant. This constant molehill of busywork can seem like a mountain of obstacles designed to keep us from what we were hired to do: sell.

The demanding manager may expect every minute of your time to be accounted for and ignore legitimate excuses for not hitting goals. Working with a perfectionist in matters of detail when you're a "big picture" kind of seller can be nothing short of a nightmare. But if you are a detailed individual yourself, you may appreciate your manager's efforts to stay informed. If you like to have constant input on how to better do your job, you may be more in synch with his style.

Suggestions for working with demanding managers

The word for working with this manager is *preparation*. Be sure you have a clear understanding of his expectations and prepare accordingly so there are less "gotcha" moments. Good advice for how to approach a demanding, perfectionist manager comes from Victor Lyndon, associate producer of *Dr. Strangelove*. In *Stanley Kubrick: Interviews,* by Kubrick and Gene Phillips, Lyndon said, "It's no good saying to Kubrick: such and such will or won't work. You've got to prove it to him, to his satisfaction, and that means you have to have all your arguments lined up very logically and precisely." So, with your manager, state your case clearly and precisely. Don't simply say, *I feel like you're micro-managing me.* Use specific examples and then explain in detail how you would perform better under a less-intense structure, then outline for him precisely what that structure would look like. Appeal to his logic with statistics and facts, not emotions.

The Actor-Turned-Director

Many directors were successful actors before turning their focus to the behind the camera. Clint Eastwood, Ron Howard, Rob Reiner, Robert Redford, and, more recently, Ben Affleck are good examples. Actors typically like working for directors who were once actors because they feel like they are more empathetic and understanding of the challenges they face. But as former actors themselves, these directors also know all of the tricks and shortcuts that actors can take. And if they have worked with slackers in the past, they may be hyper-vigilant to avoid having the wool pulled over their eyes.

The Seller Turned Manager

By far the most popular type of manager in sales, the fact that most sales managers have had some sales experience gives you a common starting point for building rapport. Problems may arise when their experience is in the distant past (this is how we did it before cell phones and e-mail), or they were promoted so quickly to management that they don't have a good sense of what it's like to sell under a variety of different circumstances.

Suggestions for working with sellers-turned-managers

Use vivid and specific examples to help your manager, not just intellectually, but emotionally recall her experience as a salesperson. Ask her what made her successful and how she approached a particular challenge that you are facing. Draw a connection between her experience and your current circumstances.

The Acting Director

Then there are those directors such as Warren Beatty, Clint Eastwood, Woody Allen, and Orson Welles who star in their own movies. Only eight times in Oscar history has someone been nominated for Best Director and Best Actor (previous names included), indicating just how difficult it is to wear two hats. When actors are well-known and established, playing both roles is likely a matter of preference; for new actors, it may primarily be a question of finance. Either way, there is likely an ego component involved (as in, *nobody can do it better than me*).

The Selling Manager

Managers who carry their own list of clients are more common in certain industries and smaller companies and they come with their own unique challenges. Often they are not as available to the rest of the team when help is required. The best seller/managers are masters of efficiency and fair in their dealings. The worst are competitive and self-seeking.

Suggestions for working with selling managers

Because this hybrid will undoubtedly have a very full plate, she will appreciate a seller who does not require a lot of hand-holding or monitoring. If you can prove that you are a valuable, trusted team player who is focused on doing his job, you can probably be assured of the freedom necessary to do it. If you do need help and are having trouble getting it, explain clearly and succinctly what is at stake and exactly how much time you need from her. Avoid getting into a competitive position with a selling manager if possible.

The Muse Director

Some actor-director pairings bring out the best in both. You begin to wonder if the director can even make a film without his muse: Pedro Almodovar and Penelope Cruz (*Volver, Broken Embraces, All about my Mother*), Tim Burton and Johnny Depp (*Edward Scissorhands, Sweeney Todd, Charlie and the Chocolate Factory*), The Coen Brothers and Francis McDormand (*Fargo, Blood Simple, Burn After Reading*). Although there is magic in these partnerships, one can't help but think that the other actors feel oddly left out. Cruz and Almodovar are also friends outside of work and share what Cruz calls a "secret language." She says of her collaboration with Almodovar: "We almost can read each other's minds…when I'm on the set, I don't feel more relaxed because he's my friend. It's the opposite…. He doesn't become less demanding because we're friends. I don't relax with him either. He's so honest and strong and specific. If something is going well, he will tell me. And if it's not, he will tell me, too. He's never rude, just honest."[12]

The Muse Manager

Muse managers have a favorite, someone who they've brought along with them or someone who has impressed them with their work. There's nothing wrong with favorites—in fact, a good manager knows that he needs to have a leader on the team who can take charge and answer questions in his absence. It's how the muse is treated that can greatly influence the rest of the team's attitude. If the muse gets all the good clients, a more favorable commission structure, or is not held to the same standards as the rest of the team, jealousy and anger flare up. If you are not the muse, your job may be more difficult and frustrating. If you are the muse, when rules are bent in your favor, you can feel uncomfortable and alienated from the rest of the team.

Suggestions for working with muse managers

If you are not the muse, don't take it out on the person who is. See if there is something you can learn from that person. Some people find it easier to ask for help from another person of equal standing. Utilize the muse to get the help you need. If you are feeling overshadowed, make sure your manager is aware of your achievements. Be your own PR person. If you are the muse, do not relax your standards. Insist that your manager be honest, direct, and fair with you at all times. As a leader, make sure you understand what he wants or expects from the team and what authority you do or do not have.

The Method Director

Wes Anderson insisted on shooting 2007's *The Darjeeling Limited* on a real moving train traveling all over India with the actors living together under one roof.[13] Sam Worthington, who plays hero Jake Sully in *Avatar*, said James Cameron would hit him or throw debris at him in order to get a reaction for the camera.[14] Hitchcock tied real birds to Tippi Hedren for the attack scene in *The Birds* and then threw others at her.[15] Inspired genius or madmen? Often the line is a fine one. Method directors typically have a "means to their madness," which, while not always obvious on set, is often brilliantly realized in the final product. If the actor trusts the director and knows that the end results will be worth it, he is typically more likely to go along with the director's bizarre requests.

The Method Manager

Emotional intelligence tests, forced bonding exercises, and sales-tech-niques-of-the month are some of the tools these managers seem to think are necessary to be different, or to succeed, or prove they are doing their job. Sometimes their ideas make sense. You have to drive the new model if you're going to talk about it convincingly. You have to bond with your co-workers if you're going to work together as a team. Other times, the relevancy or objectives are questionable, such as pub crawls or scavenger hunts, or "If you were an animal, what animal would you be?"

Suggestions for working with method managers

I am all for trying out something new if it might help me be a better salesperson or communicator, as long as it meets three criteria: It is not dangerous, it is not humiliating, and it is not illegal or immoral. I've been guilty of rolling my eyes at many an exercise I've been asked to do as a seller or an actor, but after participating, I realized that I had learned something of value. Keeping an open mind while being true to your standards is the key to working with this type of manager.

WHY DO DIRECTORS PREFER TO WORK WITH CERTAIN ACTORS?

Quentin Tarantino says he tested Samuel Jackson (*Pulp Fiction*, *Jackie Brown*) with his humor. "He got my jokes," Tarantino says. "It seems like a small thing, but if you know you're on the same page with your actor, you're going to trust each other more." Steven Soderburgh, who has worked with Matt Damon in five films to date, says of his star: "He really is one of those actors that once you've worked with him, you just want to go back. He always delivers. He's always good." The director says his favorite actors are "people who are very pleasant to work with because they come in with a great knowledge, a great deal of ammunition, and all you have to do is guide it along. It's a selfish thing." Clint Eastwood disdains needy actors. "You don't really want to go to him and say, 'I just would like to talk a little bit about the character?'" Morgan Freeman says. "He expects you to know what you're doing. And he's going to take two giant steps back and let you do it."[16]

HOW TO TAKE DIRECTION

1. Know what's expected of your role.

Ryan Gosling got it very wrong. Cast by Peter Jackson to play the grieving father in *The Lovely Bones*, Gosling gained 60 pounds before the shoot, believing that was how his character should look. When he showed up on set, Jackson told him to lose the weight. Instead he lost the role, which went to Mark Wahlberg. Gosling told the *Hollywood Reporter*: "I really believed (my character) should be 210 lbs." Gosling says of his experience with the director: "We didn't talk very much in the pre-production process. It was a huge movie and there were so many things to deal with and he couldn't deal with the actors individually. I just showed up on set and I had gotten it wrong. Then I was fat and unemployed."[17]

Don't guess what is expected of you. If you're unclear, set up a meeting to go over any vague areas in greater detail, or write out your understanding and have your manager sign off on it. Don't let a misunderstanding of your role send you to the unemployment line.

2. Focus on their strengths.

Even if you detest your boss, you're going to have to find a way to deal with the situation if you want to remain on the sales team. Review the tips for working with an uncooperative scene partner in Chapter 15. Find something your manager does that's positive: Is she always available when you have a problem? Does she give good feedback? Hold interesting sales meetings? Play great shortstop? If you can focus on the good qualities, the negative ones start to lose their strength.

3. Communicate.

Use all of the skills you've learned in this book. Build authentic rapport. Listen with your whole body. Speak with intention. Keep the lines of communication open. Try out improv techniques such as "Yes, and…" to acknowledge your manager's point of view. Collaborate on new ideas. Use the Magic If to really understand your manager's perspective.

4. Follow up.

Don't let anything fall through the cracks. Follow up on all deadlines, promised reports, or updates. You will be more credible when you have an issue if you are consistently doing the basics. Don't guess where you stand with your manager. Request a meeting and ask for feedback if you're not getting it. Discuss any performance concerns your manager might have and don't walk out until you have a specific action plan on how to address them.

5. Don't take it personally.

Remember you are playing a role (review Chapter 2) and you are being critiqued on the choices you are making in that role. It is not a reflection of you as a human being. Some directors and managers know how to gently and constructively provide feedback; others have the social skills of Attila the Hun. Look at all feedback—regardless of its delivery—and, calmly and objectively, pick out what is truthful from what is false. That attitude will go a long way toward maintaining a sane working relationship with your manager.

6. Get a coach.

Not getting the help you need? Your sales manager never has time for you, or when he does, he delivers fortune cookie wisdom? Don't let anyone get in the way of your growth. Every salesperson needs feedback—regardless of where you are in your career. Hire a coach. Sign up for a seminar. Listen to CDs. Start a sales support group.

7. Be proactive about getting your needs met.

When I was cast as the lead in a 2000 production of *The Matchmaker* (the stage version of *Hello, Dolly!*) at St. Bart's Theater in New York, I had little in common with the character. Easily 30 years younger and not-Jewish, I had never been a matchmaker for anyone, much less someone in the early 1900s when the story takes place. I kept approaching the director with my concerns. My role didn't feel right, I'd tell him. I didn't get the character. I wasn't connecting to the other characters. The director would pat me on the back, telling me I was doing fine. He would then return his attention back to staging and costuming this colorful production. He was not worried. But I was. I went to two different coaches to work specifically on this part before finding some connections that would help me create my own version of the irrepressible Dolly Levi. The play received good reviews and, even more importantly, an agent I had invited to the show came and subsequently helped me land some commercial work after that performance.

EXERCISES

1. Identify what type of manager you have using the examples given in this chapter.

2. Make a list of your manager's positive and negative qualities, as you currently see them.

3. Review Chapter 8 and the steps for how to use the Magic If. Using everything you know about your manager's given circumstances, personally and professionally, ask yourself: "What if I were in my manager's shoes?" See if you can gain a better understanding of him and a greater perspective on what you see as "negative" qualities.

4. Review Chapter 15 on working with a difficult scene partner and determine how you might apply these tools to working with your manager. Can you build on what your manager is doing right and make suggestions to make it even better? Can you offer to meet at a neutral location outside of the office to give you both a fresh perspective? How about introducing a "prop" or new sales idea to stimulate discussion?

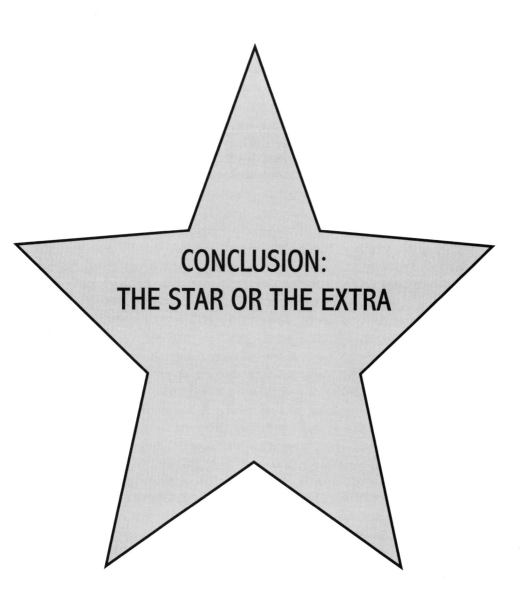

CONCLUSION:
THE STAR OR THE EXTRA

"An ounce of performance is worth pounds of promises."
~Mae West

As an extra, I've been herded into warehouses with a thousand other actors and not a chair in sight, stood in long lines for coffee, lines for costumes, lines for getting your pay card signed. I've waited hours before being called on set to do a scene that lasted 20 seconds, tops, and still not made it into the final cut. Because there is so much waiting, extras find creative ways to pass the time. They read. They knit. They do crosswords, Sudoku, even karaoke. But mostly they just talk, about acting, about getting that big break. Everybody dreams of being the actor who actually gets to *act*, the one who gets the lines, the one who gets treated with respect, the one who gets to go home with the big paycheck. Extras trade tips on shortcuts for getting ahead: buddy up to the director or the star, position yourself in front of the camera, do something unusual, ask for a line. But mostly they just go from one production to the next, professional extras, dreaming of the day when they are magically plucked out of the crowd and become the star. What about you? Are you an Extra or a Star?

Ask any professional actor and he or she will tell you that it takes practice, perseverance and commitment to get the part and deliver a winning performance. Yes, some get lucky, but the majority of working actors aren't plucked out of obscurity into the spotlight like Natalie Portman or Brad Pitt. Acting Pros aren't made overnight, and neither are Sales Pros. Professional actors don't sit and wait for the parts to come to them. They go out and find them. They prepare for them through rehearsal and practice. They hire coaches and take classes. They stay at the top of their game whether they're working or not so that they are ready when that big break comes along. Are you ready for your big break? Are you committed to doing what it takes to be a Sales Pro? Reading this book is a start; it offers you all of the tools you need to give a star-turn sales performance every time, but the magic and the motivation are within you. You have to put these techniques to use.

Follow Up With Yourself

As a seller you know the importance of following up with prospects and clients. What about the importance of following up with yourself? Reading this book, without acting on your newly acquired knowledge is like learning about a client's business, his needs, his obstacles, and not getting back to him. To paraphrase Uta Hagen, selling is intention put into action. Now that you've read this book don't just put it on the shelf, out of sight. Keep it where you can refer to it before you head into a sales scenario that you have typically responded to in an unsuccessful manner. Having trouble getting appointments? Try the exercises in Chapter 3. Missing your mojo? Re-read Chapter 5. Sitting on a deal that's been in the sales spin cycle too long? Try the closing tips in Chapter 14. Experiment with these techniques at home or socially. Dig for deeper motivation, look for drama, try out new props or substitutions. Keep doing it until you find something that works. And then do it some more. Actors build their technique one block at a time, starting with the basics, which is how this book is designed. Master one technique and build onto what you've learned with the next.

THE SALES BUG

Stand backstage before any performance, whether it's on Broadway or Broad Street and you'll feel the excitement. Actors eagerly await their chance to step into the spotlight and share themselves with an audience. Grueling auditions, long rehearsals, and bouts of stage fright are all forgotten once their feet hit the stage. When the curtain comes down on the final show, they can't wait to do it all over again. They've got the bug.

Sellers too can catch the bug. Selling is a performance and if you're not approaching it with a sense of joy and anticipation, you're missing the point. Many sellers I talk to are carrying heavier loads, worrying about their jobs, working harder for less money. Industry demands can turn your job into a production of *Les Miserables* if you let it. Adding acting techniques to your sales tool kit can put the fun back in sales. And fun is a necessary ingredient in sales, because if you're not having fun, neither is your client or prospect and your negativity can quickly become a self fullfilling prophecy. In acting this is called "being in your head" or overthinking things and taking it all too seriously. When actors get into their heads they often lose jobs, the pressure builds, and a downward spiral ensues. It is only by focusing on the joy of creating a role, sharing it with others and letting go of the results that they are able to start winning parts again. So it is with salespeople.

Selling, like acting, is a process of self-discovery and an exploration of human behavior and motivation. And it never ends. I encourage you to stay curious and willing. Always keep the creative channels open. Watch a great movie. Study powerful roles. Read classic plays. Start your own sales acting or improv group (see my Website for tips). Act like a Sales Pro and the rewards will come your way.

I leave you with this final quote from Stanislavski. It's a reminder that the business stage, like the theater, is a special place where magic can happen day after day, if we are prepared.

"Never come into the theatre with mud on your feet. Leave your dust and dirt outside. Check your little worries, squabbles, petty difficulties with your outside clothing—all the things that ruin your life and draw your attention away from your art—at the door."

~Constantin Stanislavski

APPENDIX:
SALES IN THE MOVIES

Hollywood's portrayal of salespeople is typically neither flattering nor accurate, with a few noted exceptions, but here (in no particular order) are some of the most popular films of the last few decades that give sales a starring role. The stark lack of female representation shows how little Hollywood resembles real life. Don't they know that 83 percent of the 16.1 million direct sellers in this country are female?[1]

Joe Versus the Volcano. Directed by John Patrick Shanley, Warner Brothers, 1990. Starring Tom Hanks and Meg Ryan. Delivers an inspirational message about rediscovering the magic in life and a memorable cameo by Barry McGovern as an *extremely* passionate suitcase salesman rewarded with a dream sale.

Glengarry Glen Ross. Directed by James Foley, New Line Cinema, 1992. Starring Jack Lemmon, Al Pacino, and Alec Baldwin. *"Coffee's for closers!"* Need I say more?

Tin Men. Directed by Barry Levinson, Buena Vista Pictures, 1987. Starring Richard Dreyfuss and Danny DeVito as competing aluminum-siding salesmen out for revenge. Typical Hollywood representation of salesmen as shysters.

Jerry Maguire. Directed by Cameron Crowe, Tristar Pictures, 1996. Starring Tom Cruise, Cuba Gooding, Jr., and Renee Zellwegger. Cruise's fall from the top teaches him the importance of building authentic rapport, one client at a time.

The Pursuit of Happyness. Directed by Gabriele Muccino, Columbia Pictures Corporation, 2006. Starring Will Smith and his son Jaden. Inspiring rags-to-riches story based on true story of stockbroker Christopher Gardner. It puts perspective on the obstacles most of us are faced with and redefines pursuit as purpose.

Door to Door. Directed by Steven Schachter. Turner Network Television, 2002. William H. Macy stars as Bill Porter, an irrepressible door-to-door salesman with cerebral palsy who touches his customer's lives in a number of ways during a 40-year span. A loving tribute to a remarkable salesman and a reminder of what *real* adversity looks like.

Boiler Room. Directed by Ben Younger. New Line Cinema, 2000. Starring Giovanni Ribisi and Vin Diesel. Morally bankrupt stockbrokers ruining people's lives for fast cash. High-pressure, demanding sales manager (Ben Affleck) and ethical dilemmas. Expected calls per day: 700. And you think you have it bad.

Tommy Boy. Directed by Peter Segal, Paramount Pictures, 1995. Starring Chris Farley and David Spade. Farley plays a bumbling (what else?) auto parts salesman on the road out to save daddy's company. The scenes on "don't take no for an answer" may hit uncomfortably close to home.

Love and Other Drugs. Directed by Edward Zwick, Bedford Falls Productions/Fox 2000 Productions, 2010. Starring Jake Gylenhaal, Oliver Platt, and Anne Hathaway. Based on a book by a Pfizer salesperson, this is an embellished inside look at pharmaceutical sales—before heavy regulation—and what it's like to be on the ground floor of a breakthrough product.

Planes, Trains and Automobiles. Directed by John Hughes, Paramount Pictures, 1987. Starring John Candy and Steve Martin. Even if you don't travel, you can appreciate the mishaps in this movie, as well as Candy's portrayal of Dell Griffith, shower-curtain-ring salesman extraordinaire. A fine example of endowing a small product with greater value: "This is the Michael Jordan signature earring."

The Good Girl. Directed by Miguel Arteta, Fox Searchlight, 2002. Starring Jennifer Aniston, Jake Gyllenhaal, and Zooey Deschanel as sellers in the retail hell of Retail Rodeo in West Texas. Deschanel's attempts to rouse zombie-like shoppers into action are worth seeing.

My First Mister. Directed by Christine Lahti, Paramount Classics, 2001. Albert Brooks stars as a conservative men's clothing salesman who befriends a goth girl stock clerk played by LeeLee Sobieski.

Cadillac Man. Directed by Roger Donaldson, Orion Pictures, 1990. Starring Robin Williams and Tim Robbins. Williams plays an amoral used car salesman with two days to sell 12 cars, and Robbins plays an over-reactive, jealous husband. Cue screaming and craziness.

Wall Street. Directed by Oliver Stone, 20th Century Fox, 1987. Charlie Sheen gets a lesson in shady negotiation and high-pressure sales under Michael Douglas's Gordon Gecko. Is greed really good?

The Middle. ABC, 2009. Not a movie, but a sitcom worth noting for it's more modern treatment of gender in sales. Patricia Heaton juggles a career selling cars and a high-maintenance family with often-humorous results.

American Beauty. Directed by Sam Mendes, Dreamworks, 1999. While her husband lusts after his teenage daughter's friend, Annette Benning, an uptight realtor, prepares for an open house by vacuuming in her slip and repeating to herself: "I will sell this house today."

NOTES

Introduction: The Natural
1. Thompson, "The Sexual Cowboy."
2. Pine II and Gilmore, *The Experience Economy*, 107.

Chapter 1: The Casting Call

1. Ailes and Kraushar, *You Are the Message*, 3.

2. Munn, *Richard Burton: Prince of Players*, 49.

3. Hanlon, "TV Casting – 10 Things Casting Directors Want You To Know."

4. Ibid.

Chapter 2: The Role

1. "Daniel Day-Lewis Aims for Perfection."

2. Internet Movie Database, *www.imdb.com/name/nm0000059/bio.*

Chapter 3: The Audition

1. *Dictionary.com.*

Chapter 4: The Warm Up

1. Hodge, *Actor Training*, 8.

2. Strasberg and Hethmon, *Strasberg at the Actors Studio*, 89.

3. Cohen, ed., *The Lee Strasberg Notes*.

4. Smith, "Hand Gestures Linked to Better Speaking."

Chapter 5: The Motivation

1. "Salary Wages, Pay: Actors, Producers and Directors."

2. Canfield, *The Success Principles*, 142.

3. "Dreamforce Study."

4. Watts, "4 Sales Tips for Making Contact and Avoiding 'Prospect Badgering.'"

5. Shurtleff, *Audition*, 42.

6. Ibid., 92.

7. Easty, *On Method Acting*, 24–42.

Chapter 6: The Script

1. The Mike Ferry Organization.

Chapter 8: The Scene Partner

1. Tosey and Mathison. "Introducing Neuro-Linguistic Programming."

2. Andreas and Faulkner, ed's., *NLP: The New Technology of Achievement,* 149.

3. Internet Movie Database, *IMBD.com, www.imdb.com/title/tt0089424/trivia.*

4. Williams, *A Streetcar Named Desire*, 4.

5. Stanislavski, *An Actor Prepares*, 55.

6. Ibid., 52.

7. Adler, *The Art of Acting,* 123.

8. Yahoo! Movies, *movies.yahoo.com/movie/contributor/1800035227/bio.*

Chapter 9: The Opening Night

1. Hagen, *A Challenge for the Actor*, 116.

2. Gallo, "Body Language."

3. Hagen, 101.

4. Middendorf and Kalish, "The Change-up in Lectures."

Chapter 10: The Cues

1. *Network.*

2. Hagen, 115.

3. Ibid.

4. Meisner and Longwell, *Sanford Meisner on Acting*, 22.

5. Birdwhistell, *Kinesics and Context.*

6. "The Provider's Guide to Quality and Culture."

Chapter 11: The Props

1. "Competent Communication Guide," 40.

2. "A Results Approach."

3. Middendorf and Kalish

4. "The Community Theater Dictionary."

5. Faires, "The Curse of the Play."

6. "Favorite Wicked Quotes."

7. Faires.

8. "Glossary of Technical Theater Terms."

Chapter 12: The Audience

1. Dudley and Bryant, *Behavioral Sciences Research Press, Inc.*

2. Enright, "Even Stars Get Stage Fright."

3. Cyphert. "Managing Stage Fright."

4. Moss, "Stage Fright Is the Villain Many Actors Must Upstage."

5. Hagen, 146–147.

6. Cameron. "Some Relationships Between Excitement, Depression and Anxiety."

7. Benedetti, *Stanislavski and the Actor,"* 39–42.

Chapter 13: The Cast

1. Keefe, *Improv Yourself,* back cover.

2. Duchartre, *The Italian Comedy,* 24–29.

3. Bedore, *101 Improv Games for Children and Adults,* pg 2–3.

4. Halpern and Close, *Truth in Comedy: The Manual of Improvisation,* 46–47.

5. Johnson, *The Funniest One in the Room,* 212.

Chapter 14: The Closing Night

1. English, Marketing class 377 Notes, chapter 12.

2. Canfield, *The Success Principles,* 142.

3. Ibid.

Chapter 15: The Callback

1. The Internet Movie Database, *www.imdb.com/title/tt0068646/trivia.*

2. The Internet Movie Database, *www.imdb.com/news/ni1219732/*

3. YouTube, *www.youtube.com/watch?v=y-AXTx4PcKI.*

4. Arendt, "Supporting Actors who Stole the Show."

5. Yahoo! Movies, *movies.yahoo.com/movie/contributor/1800020246/bio.*

6. TV.com, *www.tv.com/maggie-wheeler/person/1650/summary. html.*

7. Kuhn, "'Mad' for the Women…of 'Mad Men,'

Chapter 16: The Director

1. Svetkey, Behind the scenes of "Eyes Wide Shut."

2. Internet Movie Data base, *www.imdb.com/name/nm0001239/bio#quotes.*

3. "Megan Fox and Michael Bay."

4. "A Letter to Elia."

5. Brando, *Songs My Mother Taught Me,* 170–171.

6. King, "Elia Kazan, An Actor's Director."

7. Salvi, *Friendly Enemies*, 239–240.

8. Guillen, "Eli Wallach interview."

9. "Playboy Interview with James Cameron."

10. "Stories & Lifestyle."

11. The Internet Movie Database, *www.imdb.com/title/tt0081505/trivia.*

12. Bowles, Breznican, and Freydkin, "Directors and Actors."

13. Ibid.

14. Lampert, "Has James Cameron, Hollywood's Scariest Man…."

15. "The Method and the Madness of Film Directors."

16. Bowles, Breznican, and Freydkin.

17. Reeves, "Lord of the Rings Director Fired Actor…"

Appendix: Sales in the Movies:

1. "Direct Selling by the Numbers."

BIBLIOGRAPHY

Adler, Stella. *The Art of Acting.* New York: Applause Books, 2000.

Ailes, Roger, and Jon Kraushar. *You Are the Message.* New York: Crown Business, 1989.

Andreas, Steve, and Charles Faulkner, eds. *NLP: The New Technology of Achievement.* New York: Harper, 1996.

Arendt, Paul. "Supporting Actors who Stole the Show." *MSN Movies* (July 26, 2010), *movies.uk.msn.com/photos/drama/photos.aspx?cp-documentid=153124081&page=6.*

Bedore, Bob. *101 Improv Games for Children and Adults.* Alameda, Calif: Hunter House Publishing, 2004.

Benedetti, Jean. *Stanislavski and the Actor: The Method of Physical Action.* New York: Routledge, 1998.

Birdwhistell, Ray. *Kinesics and Context.* Philadelphia: University of Pennsylvania Press, 1970.

Bowles, Scott, Anthony Breznican, and Donna Freydkin. "Directors and Actors: A Special Bond, Especially for these Four." *USA TODAY.* February 14, 2010.

Brando, Marlon. *Songs My Mother Taught Me.* New York: Random House Value Publishing, 1996.

Cameron, Ewen, D., MD "Some Relationships Between Excitement, Depression and Anxiety." *American Journal of Psychiatry* (November 1945): doi: 10.1176/appi.ajp.102.3.385.

Canfield, Jack. *The Success Principles.* New York: William Morrow, 2004.

Cohen, Lola, ed. *The Lee Strasberg Notes.* New York: Routledge, 2010.

"The Community Theater Dictionary," *Community Theater Green Room: www.communitytheater.org/humor/dictionary.htm*

"Competent Communication Guide." *Toastmasters International, Inc.* (2006).

Conway, Diane. *What Would You Do if You Had No Fear? Living Your Dreams While Quakin' in Your Boots.* San Francisco: Inner Ocean Publishing, 2004.

Cyphert, Dale, PhD "Managing Stage Fright." *University of Northern Iowa, Business Communication* (2005).

"Daniel Day-Lewis Aims for Perfection." *The Telegraph* (February 22, 2008), *www.telegraph.co.uk/news/uknews/1579473/Daniel-Day-Lewis-aims-for-perfection.html*

Dead Poets Society. Directed by Peter Weir. Hollywood, Calif: Touchstone Pictures, 1989. Motion Picture.

Dictionary.com. dictionary.reference.com.

"Direct Selling By the Numbers." *Direct Selling Association* (2009), *www.dsa.org/research/industry-statistics/#PEOPLE*

"Dreamforce Study." *Insidesales.com* (2008), *www.insidesales.com/research_papers.php.*

"The Driver's Seat," *The Brady Bunch,* season 5, episode 15, directed by Jack Arnold, aired January 11, 1974 (Calif: Paramount Television), Television.

Duchartre, Pierre Louis. *The Italian Comedy.* Mineola, NY: Dover Publications, 1966.

Dudley, George W. and Trelitha R. Bryant. *Behavioral Sciences Research Press, Inc.* (2009), *www.bsrpinc.com.*

Easty, Edward Dwight. *On Method Acting.* New York: Ballantine Books, 1989.

English, Richard J. Marketing class 377 Notes, Chapter 12, San Diego State University. *www.rohan.sdsu.edu/~renglish/377/notes/chapt12/index.htm.*

Enright, Patrick. "Even Stars Get Stage Fright." *MSNBC.com* (September 12, 2007): *www.msnbc.msn.com/id/20727420/ns/health-mental_health/.*

Faires, Robert. "The Curse of the Play." *The Austin Chronicle.* (October 13, 2000.)

"Favorite Wicked Quotes." *Broadwayworld.com* (May 28, 2006), *broadwayworld.com/board/readmessage.php?thread=898683&boardid=0.*

Frare, Robert E., and John W. Connors. *Partner Selling.* Avon, Mass: Adams Media Corporation, 2000.

Gallo, Carmine. "Body Language: A Key to Success in the Workplace." *Business Week.* February, 14, 2007.

Gawain, Shakti. *Creative Visualization.* New York: Bantam Books, 1982.

Gewertz, Ken. "What are you laughing at?: Well, Richard Pryor, Woody Allen, Peter Sellers. What about S.J.Perelman?" *Harvard University Gazette.* August 22, 2002.

"Glossary of Technical Theater Terms." *Theatrecrafts.com. www.theatrecrafts.com/glossary/pages/morebreakaleg.html.*

Guillen, Michael. "Eli Wallach interview. TCM Classic Film Festival 2010: The Good, the Bad & the Ugly (1966): Onstage Conversation with Eli Wallach." May 6, 2010.

Hagen, Uta. *A Challenge for the Actor.* New York: Scribner, 1991.

Halpern, Charna and Del Close. *Truth in Comedy: The Manual of Improvisation.* Colorado Springs, Colo.: Meriwether Publishing, 1994.

Hanlon, Khara. "TV Casting—10 Things Casting Directors Want You To Know." *Instantcast.com* (November 2008): *www.instantcast.com/LearnAbout/Articles/tv_casting.*

Hodge, Alison. *Actor Training.* New York: Taylor & Francis, 2010.

"How Many Words Are There in the English Language?" *Oxford Dictionaries Online.* Oxford University Press (2010): *www.oxforddictionaries.com/page/93.*

The Internet Movie Database. *www.imdb.com*

Johnson, Kim "Howard". *The Funniest One in the Room: The Lives and Legends of Del Close.* Chicago: Chicago Review Press, 2008.

Johnstone, Keith. *Impro; Improvisation and the Theatre.* New York: Routledge, 1981.

Keefe, Joseph, A. *Improv Yourself: Business Spontaneity at the Speed of Thought.* Hoboken, N.J.: Wiley, 2002.

King, Susan. "Elia Kazan, An Actor's Director." *Los Angeles Times.* February 18, 2010.

Kubrick, Stanley, and Gene D. Phillips. *Stanley Kubrick: Interviews.* Jackson, Miss.: Univ. Press of Mississippi, 2001.

Kuhn, Sarah. "'Mad' for the Women: January Jones, Elisabeth Moss, and Christina Hendricks take charge of 'Mad Men.'" *Backstage.com* (August 30, 2010): *www.backstage.com/bso/content_display/news-and-features/e3i0cbf0f1b5c08147af5aebb6da234b81d.*

Lampert, Nicole. "Has James Cameron, Hollywood's Scariest Man, Blown £200 Million on the Biggest Movie Flop Ever?" *Daily Mail,* (December11, 2009): *www.dailymail.co.uk/tvshowbiz/article-1235154/Has-James-Cameron-Hollywoods-scariest-man-blown-200-million-biggest-movie-flop-ever.html#ixzz19olM683Q.*

Leterman, Elmer G. *The Sale Begins When the Customer Says "No."* Hillman/Macfadden Book, 1966.

"A Letter to Elia: About Elia Kazan." *PBS American Masters.* September 30, 2010. Television.

The Lives of Others (Original title: *Das Leben der Anderen*), directed and written by Florian Henckel von Donnersmarck (Munich, Germany: Wiedemann & Berg Film, 2006), Motion Picture.

"Megan Fox and Michael Bay: Our Five Favorite Moments." *MTV.com* (May 20 2010): *www.mtv.com/news/articles/1639687/megan-fox-michael-bay-our-five-favorite-moments.jhtml.*

Meisner, Sanford, and Dennis Longwell. *Sanford Meisner on Acting.* New York: Vintage, 1987.

"The Method and the Madness of Film Directors." *The Independent.* (September 13, 2009), *www.independent.co.uk/arts-entertainment/films/features/the-method-and-the-madness-of-film-directors-1839310.html.*

Middendorf, Joan, and Alan Kalish. "The Change-up in Lectures." The National Teaching and Learning Forum. Indiana University. Vol. 5, No. 2, 1996.

Mike Ferry Organization, The. *www.mikeferry.com/main/content/complementary.*

Moss, Robert. "Stage Fright Is the Villain Many Actors Must Upstage." *Newyorktimes.com.* (December 29, 1991): *www.nytimes.com/1991/12/29/theater/stage-fright-is-the-villain-many-actors-must-upstage.html*

Munn, Michael. *Richard Burton: Prince of Players.* New York: Skyhorse Publishing Inc., 2008.

The Natural, directed by Barry Levinson (Hollywood, Calif: Tristar Picture, 1984). Motion Picture.

Network, directed by Sidney Lumet (Hollywood, Calif: MGM, 1976). Motion Picture.

Pine II, B. Joseph, and James H. Gilmore. *The Experience Economy: Work is Theatre & Every Business a Stage.* Boston: Harvard Business School Press, 1999.

"Playboy Interview with James Cameron." *Playboy.com* (December, 2009): *www.playboy.com/articles/james-cameron-interview/.*

"The Provider's Guide to Quality and Culture; Topic: Non-verbal Communication." *The Manager's Electronic Resource Center. http://erc.msh.org/mainpage.cfm?file=4.6.0.htm&module=provider&language=English.*

Rackham, Neil. *SPIN Selling.* New York: McGraw-Hill, 1988.

Reeves, Tim. "Lord of the Rings Director Fired Actor for Being Too Fat." *Moviefone.co.uk* (December 3, 2010), *www.moviefone.co.uk/2010/12/03/lord-of-the-rings-director-fired-actor-for-being-too-fat/.*

"A Results Approach," *Arbonne International, LLC* (Feb 8, 2006), *www.arbonnemarketing.com/PDF/presentations/9545_CAN_ArbonneREsults_1007.pdf.*

"Salary Wages, Pay: Actors, Producers and Directors." *Job Bank USA.* (2003), *www.jobbankusa.com/career_employment/actors_producers_directors/salary_wages_pay.html.*

Salvi, Delia. *Friendly Enemies: Maximizing the Director-Actor Relationship.* New York: Watson-Guptill, 2002.

Shurtleff, Michael. *Audition.* New York: Bantam Books, 1978.

Smith, Ryan. "Hand Gestures Linked to Better Speaking." *University of Alberta's ExpressNews,* May 11, 2005.

Spolin, Viola. *Improvisation for the Theater 3E: A Handbook of Teaching and Directing Techniques (Drama and Performance Studies).* Chicago: Northwestern University Press, 3rd edition, 1999.

Stanislavski, Constantin. *An Actor Prepares.* New York: Routledge, Reprint edition, 1989.

Star Wars: Episode V—The Empire Strikes Back. Directed by George Lucas. (Hollywood, Calif: Twentieth Century Fox, 1980). Motion Picture.

"Stories & Lifestyle: Stanley Kubrick—a Director between Reality and Nightmare." *The American Dream Newsletter.* January 2005.

Strasberg, Lee, and Robert H. Hethmon. *Strasberg at the Actors Studio: Tape-recorded Sessions.* New York: Theater Communications Group, 1991.

Svetkey, Benjamin. "Behind the Scenes of *Eyes Wide Shut.*" *EW.com*, July 23, 1999. *www.ew.com/ew/article/0,,20471622_272431,00.html*

Taxi Driver, directed by Martin Scorsese (Hollywood, Calif: Columbia Pictures, 1976). Motion Picture.

Thompson, Douglas. "The Sexual Cowboy," *Daily Express.* (September 7, 1992.)

To Have and Have Not. Directed by Howard Hawks. (Hollywood, Calif: Warner Brother's Pictures, 1944). Motion Picture.

Tosey, Dr. Paul, and Dr. Jane Mathison. "Introducing Neuro-Linguistic Programming." Centre for Management Learning & Development, School of Management, University of Surrey, (2006): *www.som.surrey.ac.uk/NLP/Resources/IntroducingNLP.pdf.*

TV.com. *www.tv.com.*

Watts, Steve. "4 Sales Tips for Making Contact and Avoiding 'Prospect Badgering.' *Insidesales.com.* (August 12, 2010): *http://www.insidesales.com/insider/category/cold-calling-strategy/.*

INDEX

ABOUT THE AUTHOR

Julie Hansen combines an award-winning, 25-year sales career with her passion and experience as a professional actor into a unique and powerful selling method based on the key principles of acting and improvisation.

She is the founder of Acting for Sales, the premier coaching firm dedicated to providing sellers with innovative tools for winning business by communicating with greater confidence, authenticity and impact. Julie is a sought-after speaker and consultant for leading-edge companies that recognize the need to persuade and engage buyers in new and compelling ways in an increasingly competitive sales economy.

By applying the skills she used to win roles in national commercials, television (including HBO's *Sex & The City*), and New York stage productions to the sales model, Julie became a top sales producer in broadcasting, publishing, and real estate. She is also the former director of sales for *The National Enquirer* and *STAR* Magazine.

Julie has been featured in television and her articles have been published internationally, from *Colorado Biz* Magazine to *Entrepreneur's ThinkSales, South Africa*.

She graduated from Colorado State University with a Bachelor of Arts Degree in Business and studied acting at the Academy of Dramatic Arts and Uta Hagen's HB Studios in New York City. Julie teaches acting at the University of Denver and resides in Denver,Colorado, where she can occasionally be seen treading the boards. For more information, visit *www.actingforsales.com* or contact Julie at Julie@actingforsales.com.